W9-ANK-137

Redbirds and Rubies and Rainbows

Marlene Evans

SWORD of the LORD
PUBLISHERS
P. O. BOX 1099, MURFREESBORO, TN 37133

SWORD OF THE LORD PUBLISHERS

0-87398-720-9

Printed and Bound in the United States of America

Dedication

This book is gratefully dedicated to three of my former Sunday school teachers who will always remain in my memory as the three women having the greatest effect on my life.

. . . To my childhood teacher, Helen Zugmier, my mom, who taught me both at home and at Sunday school the meaning of the word *compassion.*

. . . To my junior high Sunday school teacher, Aunt Lela Forsyth, who was always there for me when I needed her most.

. . . To Mrs. Olin Holbrook, who gave me a deep desire to be different as a young adult in her Business Women's Sunday School Class at the Highland Park Baptist Church in Chattanooga, Tennessee.

About the Author

Mrs. Marlene Evans is the wife of Dr. Wendell Evans, President of Hyles-Anderson College; the mother of two married children; and the grandmother of one child. Mrs. Evans is a dynamic speaker who will challenge your hearts to be different women for God. She will have you laughing one minute and crying the next, while relating her experiences and teaching the entire time through Bible-taught thoughts.

Mrs. Evans is Dean of Women and a teacher at Hyles-Anderson College in Crown Point, Indiana; editor of CHRISTIAN WOMANHOOD newspaper; an author; a conference speaker for more than 20 years. She has a bachelor of arts degree in education, a master of arts degree in Christian education from Bob Jones University, a master of arts degree in education from the University of Tennessee and a doctor of humanities degree from Hyles-Anderson College. She teaches speech, psychology and Christian womanhood.

Her children are Joy Evans Ryder, married to Jeff Ryder, serving as missionaries in Inaruland, an unreached area of New Guinea (their child, Jordan Lee Ryder, was born May 31, 1986); David Evans, serving with the armed forces in Germany. His wife is Cathe Vea Evans. David and Cathe are expecting their first child to be born in July, 1988.

Introduction

Redbirds, rubies and rainbows are creations of God that have become special to me for one reason or another. As I've talked about them to ladies throughout the country, they have seemed to "spread like wildfire."

Redbirds remind me of God's love for and to us; rainbows are used of God as a token of love and trust between God and His children: "I do set my bow in the cloud, and it shall be for a token of a covenant between me and the earth" (Gen. 9:13); rubies are precious stones that can be used to remind us of what God wants us to be. ". . .for her price is far above rubies" (Prov. 31:10); ". . .for the price of wisdom is above rubies" (Job 28:18); "For wisdom is better than rubies; and all the things that may be desired are not to be compared to it" (Prov. 8:11).

This book includes my thoughts on many things God has used to help me in my Christian life. Of course, any "thing" that we look at should serve only as a reminder. Only the God who made the redbird can give us real love; only the God who made the ruby can keep us pure and make our lives worth something; only the God who made the rainbow can keep all His promises.

May the thoughts in this book serve as reminders for you to allow God to make you special and different for His glory!

Marlene Evans

Foreword

Marlene Evans is not just one of a kind—to me she's an "only"! I've known her for longer than I can believe possible and have always been amazed at her enthusiasm and ability to make others join in that exciting way she has. I can hear her now saying, "Rejoice in the Lord alway: and again, I say, Rejoice!"

I've seen Marlene when I knew she was suffering physically; yet she had that smile and faith to believe.

Marlene has accomplished much and endeared herself to hundreds of folks, and I count myself fortunate to be one of her friends.

Mrs. Lee Roberson

Table of Contents

1 – Where Are the Redbirds?

Look for the redbirds in life! They are everywhere!

I don't know how many people have said to me, "Mrs. Evans, why in the world are there redbirds all around you? Why do people give you redbird presents?"

Well, I'm going to tell you. (You know how I love to tell my "stories" over and over.)

To give you an idea of what I mean by "look for the redbirds in life," I saw a redbird on my way to the college shortly after 6:00 a.m. one morning—but it wasn't red! Let me tell you about it.

We are not used to blue herons in our area, but one had been coming to our college campus during the time I'm writing about. I came down the back roads to the college that morning, and the person driving my car slammed on the brakes and said, "There it is! There it is!" Oh, it was so pretty! The sun was just beginning to come up, and the heron was so graceful! People, that's a "redbird" in life to me, and I'll explain why I call it that.

One time I was having some real hurts and discouragements about myself. One day when I was feeling my very worst, I was driving down old Rt. 30 in the Schererville, Indiana, area (which does have a few pine trees—I love trees!), and a redbird swooped right down in front of my car. Now some of you can look out your window and see twenty-five redbirds; you wonder why I make such a big deal out of that. But I had not seen many redbirds in this area. We are an industrial area with a rather urban population. Consequently, the redbirds here are rather skittish and are not flying around just every time you might happen to want to see one. You must feed them and look for them.

You have to look for the redbirds in life here.

Now I know a family in Missouri—the Beamans—who have lots of redbirds at their house. Some of our people visit them, and one time a friend of mine counted thirty-three redbirds the weekend she was there. When something is plentiful, we don't think of it as so exciting. But I took that redbird as a sign of God's love for me. When I see a "redbird" in life, I believe He is just sending an extra reminder that He loves me.

Now, let me back up some more. I told you about the time the redbird came in front of my car. But that still isn't the beginning of the story! The story took place around Christmastime one year. On New Year's Eve I was sitting home feeling sorry for myself when I probably should have taken my hurt feelings and gone to the New Year's Eve service at my church. But since I wasn't feeling very well, I stayed home.

Then someone called me after that service at midnight or so and asked, "Are you really happy?" That someone knows me pretty well. My answer was, "I saw a redbird this morning." This person thought that was very profound. Because, of course, what it said is, "Hey, maybe I'm having troubles, but God is showing His love to me. Happy? I don't know. But joy, a deep joy that nothing can touch—even in my times of discouragement—is still down there whether I think it is or not."

My husband and I had been going to a fairly new restaurant for breakfast for several mornings in a row as a sort of treat during the holiday season. We had a little extra time since he didn't have to be in the office quite so early since students were gone. So we could sit and talk for several hours if we wanted and just enjoy each other.

For about three mornings in a row I had been facing a rather barren area which had just been landscaped. Then all of a sudden I thought I could see a redbird landing out in the snow. I mentioned it to my husband, and we thought, "Yeah, it's smoky, and there are no trees, and we are right here at the corner of Rt. 30 and Hwy. 41 at what used to be one of the busiest intersections in the nation—every truck driver used to know that corner before the interstates—and there's still a lot of traffic here." And I had surely never seen one there before.

But that morning I was just sitting there looking and I thought, *No. I'm not seeing a redbird. I have heard of people wanting water so badly in the desert that they see it—you know, a mirage. That's what this is. I'm seeing things.* But then I jumped up pointing and made a strangled noise and a big scene. My husband said, "Sit down! Sit down!" He has gotten a little used to me through the years, but people were looking at me as if to say, "What terrible thing is happening?" I just kept on pointing and struggling to say something.

Finally he looked around, and a redbird *was* sitting right where I had been looking! I don't think I had prayed for one. But since God knows our thoughts, He gives us the desires of our hearts if they're good for us. And He gave me a redbird!

I looked out there, and there was a redbird that morning out on the snow! And it was just like a picture postcard. You've seen them. The snow is beautiful and white, and the evergreen branches are covered with it—with a redbird right on the side of the picture. God gave that to *me*! I have never felt the same about a redbird since. I just feel like that's God's reminder to me even if it doesn't mean that to anyone else.

Then I started relating this. After I told the girl who called me in the wee hours of New Year's Day, I called my former Sunday school teacher, Mrs. Holbrook, in Florida and told her. She's not one of those who says, "Well, so what?" She said, "Oh, Marlene!" She got it right away. When I said with tears in my voice, "God gave me a redbird," she took right up on it.

Then after our phone conversation, she went downtown in Naples and bought everything she could find with redbirds on it. A lot was left over from the Christmas season, and she found it all—a tweeter, napkins, stationery, ornaments for my Christmas tree and many other things. This all came to me in a little package.

She played up to that little incident in my life, and she helped it become a major incident. I told it, some folks took up on it, and now others are saying, "Look for the redbirds in life."

Even though many don't even know why they are saying it, I think they get the idea just from the statement—look for the bright things, the good things, the pretty things in life.

I told my college classes; those kids told their mothers; then those women told people in their churches. Dorm supervisors taught dorm students, and now some college girls are looking for redbirds in life.

Redbirds are everywhere, people. Help others look for them, too.

Let's see what some of my other redbirds in life are.

Humorous moments can be redbirds. One day I had some students sing "Happy Birthday" to another college staff member. We had an instant happening for a few minutes. That was a redbird, and I enjoyed it.

As I went on down the hall that same day, I got another laugh. I had a bad cold at the time; and every time I "croaked" a deep hello, everyone who returned my greeting sounded worse than I did. I told Mary Purdum, one of my staff members, "I can't even be different in my colds!" Mary said, "Oh, you are different enough; don't worry about it." So I laughed, and *that* was a redbird in my life!

(When you learn to laugh at yourself, you never run out of

laughs—i.e., redbirds.) If you are constantly looking for the redbirds, you will have a great life—an enjoyable, fun and fabulous experience.

Bible verses can be redbirds. "Rejoice in the Lord alway: and again I say, Rejoice" is my life verse because it was Mrs. Holbrook's, and she quoted it so much that it stuck with me. I quote it at the end of every class I teach, figuring if students get out of Hyles-Anderson College not knowing any more verses except that one (which is highly unlikely), they *will* know Philippians 4:4 if they are in one of my classes. I can't always be with them to be a redbird when trouble happens. (And everyone, if he lives long enough, will have trouble happen sooner or later.) In fact, by the time they have an operation and someone says it's incurable cancer or incurable heart disease or whatever, it is probable that I won't even remember their names. But if I give them one verse, I will be a redbird to them when trouble does come.

Certainly a redbird isn't a verse of Scripture and a verse of Scripture isn't a redbird—but I call a verse of Scripture my redbird in life. It's just what I need when the Lord wants me to have it. He brings a verse to mind or has someone send me a card with a verse on it that will help me to rejoice. So a verse of Scripture can be a redbird in life.

Ladies, if you are looking—even though we are in a sinsick world—you will find redbirds.

I went down to Camdenton, Missouri, to visit my daughter and son-in-law when they were in missionary-candidate school. (They are now on the mission field in New Guinea.) When I asked if she had seen any redbirds, she told me no. Looking all around one morning I counted eight redbirds within about six feet from her back kitchen window! None of the people at the mission had known they were there; neither had Joy nor Jeff. I even ran into their bathroom and hopped up on the commode because I couldn't really see very well all the redbirds.

After this incident, Joy told me she had the other folks at the mission looking for redbirds. She had the thought that since mission fields won't have amusement parks, a lot of a missionary's fun will have to come from nature.

But, dearly beloved, redbirds are everywhere—if you'll only look for them! They may not really be redbirds, but look for the "redbirds" that give you a laugh or a little enjoyment. Then you can "Rejoice in the Lord alway: and again I say, Rejoice."

Short times in life are very important. They can be redbirds.

One fall Mr. and Mrs. Bud Frye, their daughter Carol, and Mary Purdum planned a short vacation together after school got started in late September. Since it was going to take them directly through Carney, Nebraska, where my dad lives now, I said, "Why don't you spend your first night with Dad?" Then I called him and told him he would be having company! (He knows them all well.)

When it was almost time for them to leave, I had the marvelous idea that it might be fun to go along to visit Dad. We checked and found that I could spend nearly two days with him and then get on a bus and come home overnight and awake refreshed in Chicago, all for the low price of $71. The free trip out was an added bonus.

I climbed up in the back of the van and slept most of the way. Dad was surprised to see me come crawling out of the van head first. I usually don't surprise him like that, but I knew he would be at home because he already knew company was coming. So it seemed a perfect time to plan a surprise visit.

As soon as I got out, Dad said, "I won't be here tomorrow. I'm planning to be gone." I assured him I would hang around anyway and have a neighbor take me to the bus station when it was time to go. Of course, we were both kidding. That was his way of saying, "I sure am surprised to see you, Marlene, and I'm so glad you're here." It was my way of saying, "I understand, Dad, that you're glad to see me and I love you, too." (You see, we speak a special language called "Zugmierese." All of the Zugmiers speak it. After all these years, I have become quite adept at both speaking and interpreting it.)

These are some of the things I got to do during the short time I was with Dad. I got to look over the whole house; read birthday cards Dad had received a few weeks earlier; read newspaper clippings he had saved for my sisters and me about things he knew we'd be interested in concerning Nebraska—our home state; I got to see old neighbors who had been friends of Mom's and Dad's for twenty-five years or more.

I enjoyed some relatively new friends who have adopted Dad—Tom and Judy Shields. (They love him and, he doesn't say this, but there is no question that he loves them, too. They're sure a redbird in my life. Judy is about the age of my youngest sister, and she looks in on Dad. If we can't get him at a time when he should be home, we call them, and they check in on him for us. She does it not as a missionary project, but because she wants to and enjoys it. When there's a game on, they take popcorn or whatever and go over to Dad's and watch the game with him. I am just so thankful for them. No one else lives near him to care for him. He is not in bad health, but he does have some things wrong with him, so it makes me feel better just knowing someone is looking in on him.)

I sat around all day Sunday dozing and talking with Dad except when I walked about five houses down to a church. I was on the couch, and he was in his recliner. We would doze awhile and talk awhile; then we fixed a sandwich and went back to dozing and talking. You can't do that type of talking when you're running around doing things.

I took a ride through the sand hills of Nebraska hoping we wouldn't get stuck or lost or run out of gas. We were looking for deer and a blue heron Dad had seen. There were quite a few deer, and we found the blue heron.

Then I talked Dad into taking me to the Ramada Inn for a

"99-cent special" breakfast. (He doesn't like to eat out.) I got to tell the waitress how important he was. We sat and talked about an hour and a half.

At home he fixed me a hamburger and a grilled cheese, and he let me eat all the wonderful pickles I wanted—ones he had canned himself.

I'm sure there were more happenings, but those are the things I now remember.

I spent about thirty-two hours traveling in order to spend about forty-five hours with Dad; and some of that time was spent sleeping during the night. You ask, "Was it worth it?" You who don't have a dad to visit, what do you think? If you had a good dad to go see, would you do it? Sure you would. It was quite a weekend.

Some people claim they must have a certain amount of time or the visit isn't worth it. But it depends on how much you put into that short amount of time you have. Sometimes you get a lot more out of the short times. My visit with Dad seemed like a long time because I spent every minute within inches of my dad. If you go home for a week or two, you think you have plenty of time. Consequently, when you are ready to leave, you realize you haven't sat down for one good visit. So if you spend your time well, a short time can be a redbird in life.

Kindness can be a redbird in life. I grew up in churches where you could sit anyplace you wanted. Because there was no growth, there was plenty of room. But one night Mary Purdum and I visited this growing church, and we unknowingly sat in the seat of one of the main couples of the church. The man had put his Bible down and gone to visit with some friends. When he came back to get his Bible, Mary sensed we were in his seat, so she said, "Will you hate us forever?" But this special, jovial Christian man said, "About 9:00 p.m. tonight I'll forget it. But from now until then, I'll be mad as fire!" We all laughed and laughed.

But that was a redbird in my life. I thank the Lord for people like him. Are you seeing what I mean?

You might call it God's blessings—you might not have to be like me and call it a redbird in life. But find them; look for them! They are not big things—not like someone calling and giving you $25,000 all at once. I'm talking about looking for those little things when you don't feel you are getting much at all.

Little things can be a redbird in life. After having a benign tumor taken out of my arm, I was advised to wear a sling for awhile. One day it was bothering me, but I didn't mention it. I just took the sling off for a few minutes.

The next day in church a lady leaned over and offered me a small square of lamb's wool, saying, "I noticed the strap was rubbing your neck raw yesterday. Try putting this under the strap at the back of your neck."

That's a redbird! Some people would say it was a little thing, but it said to me that someone cared and was discerning enough to know I had a need. She thought her way into my life.

One time I heard a husband make this comment after a mini-spectacular: "It must have been a good meeting. My wife sewed two buttons on my shirt this morning."

We have these ladies meetings and we exhort, "Be a better wife, be a better mother, be a better soul winner, etc." But how about just deciding to sew two buttons on a shirt that a husband has wanted fixed for a long time?

Another husband told me, "The meeting didn't help my wife at all. She was late for church again just as usual." I suppose he was being funny, but I thought, *If her husband doesn't want her to be late, I guess the meeting really didn't help.*

Most men just wish you would want to do what they want. They aren't macho and they don't say, "Woman, do this," and "Woman, do that." They just kind of hope that sometimes you will *want* to do what pleases them. Things that seem so little (like sewing on buttons or being on time for church) can be so big. They can be redbirds.

Special memories can be redbirds in life. You know, we should bronze every moment. Make every moment special and count it a redbird in life.

When I was small, I noticed that many families displayed a pair of bronzed baby shoes, evidently wanting to get all they could out of their baby's shoes. That is a good idea.

But if we think that is good, why don't we bronze every moment we have, especially the good moments? Some of us bronze every bad moment. We hold onto it, look at it, nurse it, think about it, put it up to look at, talk about it, dwell on it and remember every bad thing that ever happened. But we can't quite remember the good things. Why don't we bronze every good moment? There are so many in everyone's life, no matter what your situation.

When Joy and David were little, we most always took a trip to Nebraska around Christmas Day. There was quite a crowd. My dad's dad (Grandpa), my Aunt Edna who was retarded, Aunt Lela and Uncle Carl would come from Wymore, Nebraska, to Axtell where Mom and Dad had a small motel. Katherine, my younger sister, was still at home a lot of those years and was still in the area. My middle sister Doris and her husband Jerry were in education like my husband and I. We were not in administration at that time, so we had the whole two weeks off. Then Katherine married Dick, their child Beth came along, Doris and Jerry had Mike, and we had David and Joy. Among us, we kept the motel jumping.

One morning as I was sweeping the motel office, I cast a moment in bronze. I can see it exactly right now. I told myself that this was not always going to last. I admonished myself to enjoy every second of all the generations under one roof for a giant house party. Think of it! Grandpa Zugmier was still alive; my second closest parenting people, Aunt Lela and Uncle Carl, were there; a favorite aunt, Aunt Edna, was there; and Dad and Mom had a ten-room motel to accommodate us all. There weren't many guests at that time of year, so we could all spread out.

I said to myself, *Marlene, you are fortunate. It just so happens that all of this is possible, and I hope you know what you have.* (I talk to myself a lot!) Then I drank it in as best I could.

As I went from the kitchen into the large living room, I'd stop a second to soak up the atmosphere. It was almost like a Norman Rockwell scene. The Norman Rockwell Thanksgiving picture shows just one meal—we had many such meals when we'd put all the tables together.

Now there were times when Grandpa would get upset. He smoked, so there was smoke in the house. And he had a leg off and the nerve endings would hurt him sometimes. Aunt Edna went through some nervous times. And one time we all took turns getting desperately sick with the flu. So, realistically, I know there were bad times—lots of work and times of people not feeling well—but all I can remember now are the magical moments that I cast in bronze. Cast your redbirds in bronze!

I knew it wouldn't last. I wasn't being cynical, but people do have to go on to be with the Lord. One by one they—Uncle Carl, then Grandpa Zugmier, and then my mom—left us. Then Aunt Lela couldn't travel anymore. Dad no longer owned the motel, and when he retired, he moved from Axtell to Carney. New grandkids have been added; my kids are now coming home to my house for the holidays. The scene keeps shifting, but we should still bronze each moment.

After our reunions I remember all too well pulling away from the motel with my family. I'd wave and cry for at least ten miles as I left that group who meant so much to me. Each time we parted I figured it might be the last time for one of them. I am not sorry they're in Heaven, but I'd like to hug them again.

One year when Joy and Jeff had just pulled out of my driveway after a visit, as I went back in the house David took me off to the kitchen to "show me something." It was an obvious and sweet attempt to dilute my hurt and loneliness. I cast the moment in bronze.

Sometimes we cast a hurtful moment in bronze when we could do something to avoid it. I once had a terrible twenty-four hours when David left to go back to school. That day was also one cast in bronze, but I didn't want to repeat it again. So the next time any of my children left me, I planned things to do after the big event.

Once, when Joy and Jeff had departed, I planned several things to do to force me to get my mind off their leaving. I did some work things. Then David and his girlfriend, who is now his wife, went out to eat with me. No use to go to bed crying when one child was still home, you see.

We sometimes cast more hurtful moments than good moments when we could avoid doing so by looking for the redbirds in the midst of our hurtful moments.

There will also be times when we cast a moment in bronze out of fear. When David was six years old, one winter day my friends Annie Ruth McGuire and her mom, Mrs. Reid, took their Ray and my Joy and David to Gatlinburg, Tennessee. Everyone, including David, rented skis. I thought it would be a good opportunity for him to learn to stand up on them.

I was in the rental lodge and turned to look out the window only to see my David being put into a ski lift to go to the top of the mountain. I stood frozen, no longer able to communicate! The moment was cast in bronze. We did get him down from the mountain without his having his first skiing experience, but that moment will be cast in bronze forever.

Since there will be moments that aren't redbirds, let's be sure we capture all the good moments in bronze, too. Every time you see something that you know fits the "redbird" description, cast it. Call it whatever you want—blessing of God, casting a moment in bronze, a redbird in life—but be sure you cast it!

Are you counting the tiny things and short times? Are you counting everything? Count them and go over them one by one. And cast them in bronze. Look for the redbirds in life, and you'll be able to "Rejoice in the Lord alway: and again I say, Rejoice."

2 – Rubies

I love the sparkle and bright color of rubies and have been intrigued by them ever since I was a little girl sitting on my dad's lap studying his ruby ring Mom had given him.

A few years ago I again became enamored with rubies when my husband and I were visiting the church of Dr. and Mrs. Tom Berry in Maryland. Mrs. Berry was teaching a ladies' group in which she encouraged all the ladies to be those whose price is far above rubies. During this study the husbands began purchasing pieces of jewelry with at least a ruby chip somewhere in them. I shall never forget that.

At the Spectacular commemorating the 10th anniversary of *Christian Womanhood,* the lady students, staff and faculty presented me with a beautiful ruby and diamond ring. *Christian Womanhood* saw to it that Pat Hays, the assistant editor, also received a ruby ring.

Every time I glance at my ring I think, *Is* my price far above rubies today? It's a constant reminder to do my best for the Lord, my family and the work He has given me.

Ladies from Dr. Gary Herring's church in Uniontown, Pennsylvania, took note of what happened at the Spectacular and gave Mrs. Herring a gorgeous ruby and diamond ring about one year ago.

At the 1986 Spectacular, we were thrilled to put a ruby and diamond ring on the finger of Mrs. Jack Hyles, our preacher's wife. She is one whose price definitely is far above rubies.

I have learned through the grapevine that Linda Stubblefield, *Christian Womanhood* business coordinator, recently saved her money and chose a pretty ruby ring for one of her Christian heroines.

If you want to challenge your Sunday school teacher, daughter, sister or friend with a piece of jewelry, you don't have to have access to the U.S. mint to do so. You can purchase earrings, necklaces, pins or bracelets, asking for a couple of tiny rubies which are real but quite inexpensive.

In our area we go to a jewelry manufacturer, tell him how much money we have, and watch him put together something very pretty for a lot less money than we would pay at a mall.

The price of the ruby isn't the issue; it's the reminder behind it.

". . .for the price of wisdom is above rubies" (Job 28:18).

"For wisdom is better than rubies. . ." (Prov. 8:11).

". . .her price is far above rubies" (Prov. 31:10).

3 – Rainbows

Have you ever looked out at the countryside on a rainy day only to be suddenly surprised with a beautiful rainbow—one that had every hue? I think we'd be surprised how often those rainbows are there if we but looked for them.

In this old sin-sick world, things can get to looking mighty dreary at times—if we have our eyes on the clouds. But if we will look closer, God will show us a rainbow in the midst of the clouds. I consider the rainbow a token of God's love for me, a symbol that He cares even in the midst of my pain. And He always gives me one just when I need it the most.

Now when I say, "Look for a rainbow," I don't mean that you will always get a literal rainbow. I am saying that you should look for something God has sent to remind you that He is still your God and has everything under control.

When you are hurting, remember to keep your eyes off the clouds and look for the rainbows: God has given you many if you'll just look for them!

"I do set my bow in the cloud, and it shall be for a token of a covenant between me and the earth" (Gen. 9:13).

4 – One Step at a Time

One step at a time, only one step at a time.
This is the way the Lord will lead you, one step at a time.
Take that one step carefully; walk that one step prayerfully;
This is the way to victory, one step at a time.

—Dr. Sidney Cox

I suppose Dr. Cox's chorus would have to be one of my favorites, if not my favorite. To me, it is deep! It has meat. It is the formula for victory. Perhaps you consider it simply a little ditty with nice words. But there's nothing simple about it. It's the most difficult thing I have ever had to learn. I will never completely get it. If I could learn it, I'd never be frustrated again. The truth of these words is the reason for both gain and loss. Since "the steps of a good man are ordered by the Lord" (Ps. 37:23), and if that good man (or woman) takes that one step at a time, victory will come! It is that deep, yet that simple.

One Step at a Time Causes Us to Win Over Problems

We tend to want a big magical formula for our problems, and we feel cheated when we're given just one little step to take. We feel so cheated we disparage the advice and go to some place or someone who will give a more complex solution, one we're sure not to be able to follow but one we can admire while we keep failing.

We stay fat because we worry over big weight losses tomorrow instead of doing something about a half-pound loss today. We say, "Big deal! What's a half a pound?" It's the first and only step we can take today. That's what it is.

We spend a lifetime feeling pressure over debts because we don't pay off a little bit of the debt this week. We say, "How will $10 help on that bill when I owe hundreds?" It's the one step you can take now!

We often say, "Take that first step out into the aisle, and it will be easier to take the rest." Many a person puts off a public profession of Christ for years or forever because he or she does not know the philosophy of "one step at a time."

The devil and the world's philosophy have us all messed up! The world tells us things like, "There's no use going to church if you don't mean it. You wouldn't get anything out of it anyway." That's a lie! Many an insincere person has accepted Christ after taking that first step of going to a church. Hundreds of times I've wanted to stay home when church time came, yet I have received as many blessings and helps on the "not-wanting-to-go days" as I have on the "want-to-go days."

The world, even the Christian world, will also tell us not to go soul winning unless we sincerely want to do so. I've won as many souls when I didn't want to go as I have when I wanted to go. As many souls are still living for the Lord of those won when I didn't want to go as when I wanted to go. Take that first step of getting out your door, and you'll probably begin wanting to go.

Many an alcoholic wants to be sure she (yes, "she," for more women than ever before are hooked on liquor!) can take the fifteenth step of getting off drink before she takes the first step. She is definitely not capable of taking any step but the first step; therefore, she will be hooked for as long as she waits for the strength to take all the steps at once.

One Step at a Time Will Help Us Win Over Worry!

We wringers of hands don't really want a step to take! We want to continue our hand-wringing and feel hostile toward anyone who acts as if there's something simple to do about any problem. We really feel our problem is not understood and that we are being insulted by being given only one step to take.

One time a young friend of mine was bemoaning the fact that her mother had just married a man of whom she could not approve. In fact, the girl had barely met him. She didn't really know anything about him except his reputation—which was poor.

The daughter was also getting married, and the mother was insisting her new husband be in the wedding pictures. Oh, me! Oh, my! What to do! She didn't want him in those pictures. When she talked to the preacher about it, he said, "Have some pictures made with him in them; rearrange the group, and have some without him. Then send your mother the pictures she wants." It was so simple that it was flabbergasting!

We make our own big problems. For that matter, if we do have a really big problem (which is rare), it has to be broken down and solved simply—one step at a time.

In 1980 I wrote a story which illustrates the "one-step-at-a-time" principle. Let me share it with you.

> Right now I'm on a big 747 plane over the Atlantic Ocean. My husband and I have just enjoyed the gift of a week in England and Scotland and are returning home. He told me something really good. I hadn't bugged him with questions for which he had no answers.
>
> On a trip like this, there are a million things to ask ahead of time. This has been especially true because we have been completely on our own, with no guide and in no tour group. As soon as we arrived in London we picked up a rental car and did what we "jolly well" felt like doing for a few days.
>
> Now, my husband had made advance arrangements, but there is no way to picture just how everything is going to be. You have to take the first step before you can take the second

> one. Just this morning we had to take one step at a time as we reached Heathrow Airport in what should have been ample time, only to find scores who had stood in line for several hours.
>
> I started to ask the inevitable before I regained enough sense to shut my mouth. I didn't want my husband to retract his statement about my not bugging him! Here are some of the questions I had in mind: "Do you think we'll make it?" "Will they let us on through if they know what plane we're taking?" "Do they have to look through our luggage?" "How long will that take?" "If we don't make it, when will there be another plane?" "Will we have to call home?" "How will we ever get an international operator?" "How will we ever pay for it?" "What will we do today?" "What time is it at home?" etc., etc., etc. I'm very imaginative this way. (Actually, we can take in the answer only one step at a time.) Obviously, we did make it, but I now have a new set of questions!

I was good one other time, too. (I always have been better at the big situations than at the little ones. Finding my way to my sister's house in Young America—one of those suburban developments where there's 75th Place, 75th Avenue, 75th Street, 75th Court and 75th Drive—absolutely panics me.) Let's get back to that one other good thing I did!!

One time Dr. Billings, then president of Hyles-Anderson College, came by the classroom where I was teaching and asked, "Would you like to go to London today with Dr. Evans for the Conference of Fundamentalists? I just thought of it, and the students would like to pay your way."

I'm sure I gave my usual blank stare at such a turn of events and acted unappreciative. Those things take awhile to sink in on me. Now at that time I'd barely been across the borders into Mexico and Canada. That was the extent of my world traveling.

Really, the only catch was that my husband was already scheduled to leave for London that very night, but I had two kids and several college classes to arrange for before I could leave! I did not have and had never had a passport, plus I had no birth certificate or passport pictures. However, it was ONLY 10:00 a.m., and we didn't have to leave until 7:00 THAT EVE-

NING! I thought maybe nine hours would do it, so I proceeded to step one: calling the Chicago passport office. They laughed and said I couldn't make it.

Next step: Decide whether or not to try.

Step three: Make decision to start work on my passport for future trips and just take my things along in case everything clicked for the night trip. Important: Do all I can to get on 7:00 p.m. plane with husband, but don't let self know I'm really thinking I might make it. This helps avoid crying all night if I don't make it.

Step four: Call Dage County, Nebraska, and ask the clerk to wire a copy of my birth certificate. I was told all that had been moved to Lincoln, Nebraska. I called Lincoln. I had to wire $3.45 before they could wire the birth certificate. I told them I'd never make it. I said this Nebraska girl had a chance to go to London to see the queen (not really)! I told them all about playing "London Bridge" in yards in Blue Springs and Wymore, Nebraska. Could they take up a collection for me in their office? I would wire money right away but would never stand a chance if they didn't wire the birth certificate right then! I even promised to send gifts from London! I told them they could trust a Nebraska girl. They laughed, but they said they would send the birth certificate to the Chicago passport office!

Step zero: Meanwhile, at the college, Linda Meister is in action packing a suitcase for me, making arrangements for kids, classes and helping me find a way to Chicago. I told my husband I would be at the airport at 7:00 p.m. if I was going and "good-bye" if I wasn't there. Then I did a few hundred other things.

Step five: Find a girl at the college whose mother just came, to take her to their Chicago home for a visit. Arlene Beck and her mom knew Chicago. Mrs. Beck worked right downtown by the passport office. (Oh, by this time it is way into the afternoon because I had an 11:00 a.m. girls' chapel session at which to speak.)

They took me to Chicago and Arlene went into the passport office with me. There we found out that the office closed at 4:00 p.m., I needed to get pictures made across the street, and the wire had to be delivered from the Chicago Telegraph Office to the passport office; it could not be called in even if it was there.

Step six: Arlene says, "I know where the nearest telegraph office is. I'll go wait and bring it back to the passport office."

We called Western Union from the passport office. The Western Union person laughed angrily and told us how many thousands of telegrams come through their office. I told them I just wanted one! (They didn't care about a Nebraska girl going to London!) While Arlene was gone, I had my picture made, and then I returned to wait at the passport office.

Step seven: The man at the passport office said if Arlene wasn't there with the telegram by 4:00 p.m., he was closing! I dejectedly, but not disappointedly (I hadn't planned on going anyway!), picked up my umbrella (for London showers) and slowly turned to go. The man said, "Okay, I'll stay until 4:15 p.m." He locked the doors. I wondered how Arlene would know I was in there. At 4:12 p.m. Arlene knocked. I let her in.

Step eight: I ate lunch at 5:00 p.m. and caught the airport shuttle bus in front of a hotel.

Step nine: I was at the right gate at O'Hare Airport with passport in hand at 7:00 p.m. I told my husband, "Hello," and we left for London!

Take one step, then another, and just see where it gets you, okay? Don't worry if you don't finish all the steps each time. Start again.

One Step at a Time Causes Us to Win. . .or Lose!

We don't need the courage to face life's big tests. What we need is the courage to meet life's little tests. We need the courage to follow a regular routine, the courage to stick to our plans, the courage to keep the petty irritations of the day from blocking our efforts, and the courage to keep on going hour after hour. We need to remember that it isn't the big trees that trip us as we walk through the forest but the vines on the ground, the exposed roots and the low underbrush.

This philosophy will work for good or evil. If only we understood the depth of the truth, "one step at a time," we would avoid almost every loss in our lives.

Dr. Bob Jones, Sr., used to say, "Back of every tragedy in human character is a process of wicked thinking."

The Word of God says, "My heart was hot within me, while I was musing the fire burned: then spake I with my tongue" (Ps. 39:3).

We don't abuse (abusing does not mean applying scriptural discipline) our children overnight. First, we let ourselves become exhausted, or we allow ourselves to think what we could be doing if we didn't have the kids. Then we take on too much outside the home or get involved in some sinful pleasure. Then we scream and yell, we yank INSTEAD of taking time for teaching, guiding and giving good spankings on the bottom. Then we actually physically abuse our own children!

People say they don't understand how a mother can really abuse her child. I can. It's one step at a time. Yes, it's one step at a time, winning or losing.

Others say, "How could a woman who has seemed fairly decent leave her children for another man?" It's one step at a time. She didn't plan to leave her children when she went out for an innocent lunch with a man at work. By the way, going out to lunch wasn't the first step with her. The first step was not watching and planning and taking heed. Then, there was the conversation that became a little too familiar, and you may know the rest. By the time she leaves her home, she's no longer able to think clearly; so, of course, she can leave her children.

I heard Dr. Russell Anderson say once that he never called another man's wife by her first name. I'm sure many of you find that odd. He's just aware of the "one-step-at-a-time" principle.

Dr. Lee Roberson is so careful about "one step at a time" that Lee Ann, his daughter, used to say, "Daddy wouldn't pick me up in the car if it were raining and he passed me walking down the street." I'm sure many of you laugh, but let me say this: as far as I know, Chattanoogans who might like to have had something to say, have been unable to find anything to say against that great man! He plans it so they won't have anything to twist.

Some of you write about tragedies in your daughters' lives and you ask, "How did it happen?" I don't know the details—the name of the boy, the motel or the home—but I can tell you it happened "one step at a time." Some of you thought that holding hands was cute when your girl was thirteen or fourteen years old. Others didn't think it was too wrong for your girl to wear shorts or other skimpy or form-fitting clothes. In fact, you wanted your daughter to be "in style." You even told her she looked sexy. And then there are those of you who actually laugh over the idea of a chaperone.

I'm not saying you can be 100% guaranteed what your daughter will do. I am saying you have 100% control over what attitude you take toward these things. I am not saying that every girl who holds hands will get into trouble. I am saying there are very few girls who get into trouble who haven't held hands, then necked, then petted before they got into trouble. Excuse me, but the phrase "get into trouble" is as true as it ever was. The world laughs at that phrase; but I call abortion, disease, unwanted children and emotional and psychological disturbances "trouble." So do the ones who go through it!

Whether we're going the good or bad route, winning or losing, it's always "one step at a time," and it's always progressive. We don't stand still.

One Step at a Time Will Help Us Teach!

"One step at a time" will not only help us teach, but it's the only way we can really teach. We can talk another way, but we cannot teach any other way. I'm afraid many who are teachers of Sunday school children, of bus kids, of school students or of those in our own home are only glorified babysitters. There are very few real teachers!

Dr. Jack Hyles is a real teacher! On Wednesday nights he reads the Bible to us, then he tells us the story. After that, he has us tell it back to him. Sometimes he acts it out. Then he reviews, after which we tell it to him as a group once again as he asks questions of all of us.

He makes it simple so that my husband, who is a Ph.D., can understand it! He makes it simple so my retarded friend, Susie Taylor, can tell the whole story on her own! I am writing these statements very seriously and am not in a joking mood at all. (Sometimes those who have studied complex material find it almost impossible to grasp practical truth.) My husband says he learns so much from the "one-step-at-a-time" teaching of Dr. Hyles. I've heard Susie give intricate stories of books of the Bible. (I've also noticed that both of them learn the truths well enough to live by them.)

Dr. Hyles has a brilliant mind and knows the Bible as very few men know it, but he knows about teaching "one step at a time." That is why we go out of our church doors wanting to do something. "One-step-at-a-time" teaching "takes" and it "sticks"!

When you teach your child to tie his shoes, you don't say, "You just take it like this, and do like that, and fix it up this way and there you have it." No, there you don't have it! You say, "Let's just learn one step today, and I'll do it for you. Then, you do it. Then, I'll do it again."

We still have the idea that we have to cover all the material. We do need to cover the material, but not if we're not teaching it! Where are we going so fast? I'll tell you where we're going. Nowhere! Let's teach one step at a time. It's the only way!

Make Your Resolutions One Step at a Time

Perhaps you are one of those who has said, "I'll make no New Year's resolutions. I never keep them, so why make them?"

Now think back over those resolutions. Were they something like this? I promise to: (1) lose 50 pounds in three months, (2) win 50 souls in the same three months, and (3) keep a beautiful home, good children and a happy husband while taking on four new projects in those same three months.

The trouble is, none of the above resolutions include the "how." Instead, say this: "I am going to my doctor to ask for a sensible way to begin weight loss. I will join a soul-winning club or find a soul winner to teach me how to win souls. I will clean out the freezer and refrigerator today and tackle the rest of the kitchen tomorrow." It doesn't sound as glamorous or dramatic, but it works!

"One step at a time" works in winning, in losing, in worrying and in teaching. It just works—that's all!

One step at a time, only one step at a time.
This is the way the Lord will lead you, one step at a time.
Take that one step carefully; walk that one step prayerfully;
This is the way to victory, one step at a time.

—Dr. Sidney Cox

5 – The Greatest Gift

When Christmas approaches, I think about gifts. Let me share my thoughts with you.

The drudgery of buying gifts comes into play when you have no idea what in the world to get for someone. All the advertisements scream, "Buy Product X for the person who has everything!" But Product X never seems to suit the people I know, and they're not the people who have everything anyway.

Everyone says, "I want to buy something different and unusual for my people this year." Just about the time I finally think of something different and unusual, it's taken off the market and the clerk says, "You won't find that anywhere." I always wonder how she knows I won't find it anywhere. Has she traveled the Chicago area for that item herself?

The sales promotion crowd tries to hurry me by saying, "Buy today and get this free gift!" What's that supposed to mean? The dictionary listing of *gift* reads: **"something that is given."** Now, if I have to buy something to get the gift, is it really a gift?

I've heard people accuse others of being "Indian givers"—ones who take back what they once supposedly gave. Among the grade-school set, this is positively criminal. I guess they are right in their evaluation.

Christmas buying comes earlier every year. It's just so commercial. I have a hard time even enjoying it anymore.

You say, "Marlene, you're awful! You're making Christmas sound bad. I don't like such negative and gloomy talk."

Let's Shift Gears!

Okay, you're right, so come along with me as I shift gears and do some substitute thinking. I'm always having to practice putting out the bad thoughts with Philippians 4:8 thinking anyway: "Finally, brethren, whatsoever things are true, whatsoever things are honest, whatsoever things are just, whatsoever things are pure, whatsoever things are lovely, whatsoever things are of good report; if there be any virtue, and if there be any praise, think on these things." It's just natural for me to think one wrong thought and have hundreds of wrong thoughts tumble in on me.

Here we go!

Don't you love to plan and shop for a gift you know is just right for someone? Everything about the gift is fun as you anticipate the pleasure it will bring.

I'm going to think of real gifts—ones that won't be taken back; ones that won't be pushed on me. They will be different and unusual, and they definitely will suit the people to whom I'm giving them.

I'd Like to Give Alice Fay Hands and Feet

I'll never forget the Christmas Miss Harlow and I ventured into town to buy gifts for our orthopedically handicapped children at the Mary Ann Brown Center in Chattanooga, Tennessee. As we browsed around, we were approached by a clerk who asked about our needs and tried valiantly to make good suggestions. Until we noticed the horrified look on her face, we hadn't realized how callously hard our remarks were sounding. Alice Fay was a fact of life with which we lived!

The conversation had gone something like this:

Clerk: "How about getting all the girls some of these little houseslippers with animals on them?"

Teachers: "Oh, yes, they are cute. Let's get those! Oh, no, Alice Fay doesn't have any feet—those won't work."

Clerk: "What about buying little rings with appropriate birthstones for each girl?"

Teachers: "Let's get those! Oh, but we can't because Alice Fay doesn't have hands."

I won't try to tell you that these exact words were said; but before we left, the saleslady also suggested barrettes and singing toothbrushes to which we had to reply something to the effect that Alice Fay didn't have hair or teeth.

Until I saw the look of disbelief and then pity which crossed the face of the clerk, I had almost forgotten the tragedy of Alice Fay. As teachers, we had to block out a few problems as we laughed with Alice Fay about how she could wear a tight gold bracelet on her wrist for a wedding band someday . . . scold her for beating all the other kids as she learned to walk (or run) the monkey bars with her arms.

She must be very adult now. She was fitted with a wig and dentures a long time ago. I wonder how she's doing. I wish I could give her hands and feet for Christmas. I doubt that I wish it enough to give my own to her, if it were even possible, but I would really love to give a Christmas gift of hands and feet to Alice Fay.

I'd Like to Give Aunt Edna a High Seat in Heaven!

When I was a little girl, I really looked forward to going to Grandma and Grandpa's house on Christmas Day. Actually, that is an understatement because I anticipated the event to such an extent that I was sometimes sick by the time I got there. I'd have to go to the bedroom to lie down a little bit in hopes of quieting my stomach—which was turning flip-flops.

Someone else at Grandpa's house sometimes retreated to the bedroom, and that was Aunt Edna. When she was in the third grade of school, she fell victim to polio and consequently suffered a speech impediment and other damage which in those days resulted in her being different and not having a formal education.

Aunt Edna and I had good times together. I think she liked me a lot, and I know I liked her. Even into my college and married years, I played a game that would never fail to make her laugh. I pulled an imaginary dog around on a leash—training it, giving it rest stops, feeding it and doing anything else that came to my feeble mind. She'd wipe the tears from her eyes as she'd cry, "Why, Marlene, you 'clazy' thing. There's no dog!" I was so glad I could be "clazy" if it helped to provide Aunt Edna a little fun. It seemed as if she always sat back away from everyone. My grandparents loved her and were trying to protect her, as everyone did in those days.

I always wanted to give her things and do things that would make up to her for what she was missing, though I never knew what to do.

When she died, I flew to Nebraska to attend the funeral. Some of the thoughtful girls who worked with me at the time gave me a fall corsage to wear on the airplane. They knew my aunt was special, and the corsage told me so.

After everyone left the grave, I placed the wilted corsage, which I was carrying in a bag, on her grave and said, "Lord, let her know that if I care more for others because of watching her take a back seat for forty years, if I do something that helps others, she probably has had something to do with it."

Aunt Edna, I couldn't give you good speech and the ability to read and write. I didn't even know what little trinket to give you to make you glad.

This Christmas I'm asking Jesus to please give you a high seat in Heaven.

The Perfect Gift

I know something better than hands and feet for Alice Fay

or a high seat in Heaven for Aunt Edna! I get so excited when I think about this gift because it's different and unusual. It suits the person who has everything. No one will take it back. No one has to do anything to get it. And it can't be pushed onto anyone. Let me tell you about it.

God made a world and then became lonesome for fellowship. He said, "Let us make man. . ." (Gen. 1:26). That man was Adam. A wife was made for Adam—right from his own rib. When Adam and Eve disobeyed God, He could no longer fellowship with them because He could not look on sin.

God wanted fellowship with us, but He could no longer have it; so He made a plan by which the sins of man could be covered. He sent His only Son to earth to die for man. As we accept Jesus' blood to cover our sins, we are accepting the perfect gift—salvation through Jesus Christ our Saviour.

God holds His Son, Jesus Christ, out to you and says, "He's My Gift to you. Take Him, won't you?"

God's Plan for Saving Sinners

1. God sent His Son into the world that He might take the sinner's place. When Jesus died on the cross as God's Lamb, He took the punishment that belonged to the sinner.

John 3:16,17—"For God so loved the world, that he gave his only begotten Son, that whosoever believeth in him should not perish, but have everlasting life. For God sent not his Son into the world to condemn the world; but that the world through him might be saved."

John 1:29—"Behold the Lamb of God, which taketh away the sin of the world."

2. When we acknowledge ourselves to be sinners and take Jesus Christ as our Saviour, God gives us a new nature. We are born from above.

John 3:3, 7—"Verily, verily, I say unto thee, Except a man be born again, he cannot see the kingdom of God. Marvel not that I said unto thee, Ye must be born again."

3. By our acceptance of Jesus Christ as Saviour and Lord, we receive eternal life.

John 1:12—"But as many as received him, to them gave he power to become the sons of God, even to them that believe on his name."

John 3:36—"He that believeth on the Son hath everlasting life: and he that believeth not the Son shall not see life; but the wrath of God abideth on him."

John 5:24—"Verily, verily, I say unto you, He that heareth my word, and believeth on him that sent me, hath everlasting life, and shall not come into condemnation; but IS passed from death unto life."

When you read these verses, you will understand that this new life is a gift: "He gave." It is eternal: "Hath everlasting life."

Are you, as a lost sinner, willing to receive Jesus Christ as your Saviour, believing that He was God's Lamb, that He took your place when He died on the cross, and that His shed blood was a sufficient atonement for your sin?

Are you willing to confess Him before men as your Saviour?

If so, sign your name below and keep this book always as a reminder of your decision and your declaration.

Your signature: ________________________________

Then confess Jesus Christ to be your Saviour. Be bold and frank always in acknowledging Him as both Saviour and Lord, as did the Samaritan woman in John 4:28,29 and 39:

"The woman then left her waterpot, and went her way into the city, and saith to the men, Come, see a man, which told me all things that ever I did: is not this the Christ? . . . . And many of the Samaritans of that city believed on him for the saying of the woman, which testified, He told me all that ever I did."

6 – Love Is...

Valentines—hearts—romance—beauty—flowers—perfume—cupids—lace: But is this love?

I don't know! Love is something I can't begin to grasp. I'm afraid I don't always recognize it even when I actually see it. Songwriters say, "Love is a many-splendored thing," and, "Love makes the world go 'round," and, "Without love you ain't nothin' at all"; and although I believe some of this, I'm not sure the writers know anything more about love than I do.

Love Is...

We probably know some things love is. Remember those sayings, "Happiness is..." and, "Love is...." Here are a few things they portray love to be:

Dr. Jack Hyles has said, "Love asks, 'How much can I do?' not, 'How much do I have to do?' and, 'How much can I give?' not, 'How much do I have to give?' "

In 1968, a young lady at Tennessee Temple described what love can do:

Love, although intangible, is the most real of realities—
Although it cannot be touched, it can be felt.
Although it cannot be seen, it can be known.
Although it cannot be bought, it can be given.
Where there is sorrow, love gives comfort.

Where there is discouragement, love gives hope.
Where there is loneliness, love befriends.
Where there is weakness, love gives strength.
Where there is discontentment, love brings peace.
Where there is emptiness, love fills.
Love, human love, gives meaning to life.
But love, God's love, gives Life.

—Sue (Farrar) Adkisson

Love Is Eternal

Abraham Lincoln had the words "Love Is Eternal" engraved in his wedding band. That thought seems to verify several statements which keep going around in my head: "A friend is one who knows all about you and loves you just the same," and, "You can't do anything bad enough to cause me to stop loving you."

Of course, we know by Ephesians 4:32, "And be ye kind one to another, tenderhearted, forgiving one another, even as God for Christ's sake hath forgiven you," that learning that which is bad about a person or receiving harm from him is absolutely no reason at all for withholding our love. God, for Christ's sake, has forgiven us! What in the world could anyone do to us worse than what we've done to God?

Love Is Not...

If love is a give-and-take thing depending upon the recipient's goodness and sweetness, you probably don't love. I've heard Dr. Jack Hyles say, "Love doesn't depend upon the condition of the object of that love but upon our condition."

Now, just think a minute. Could you stop loving your son? What could he do which would make you stop loving him? When you received that boy into your home, you committed yourself, as you did in marriage, for better or for worse.

Oh, that we would love all people that way! Then we would be approaching obedience to the Scripture.

"Beloved, if God so loved us, we ought also to love one another. No man hath seen God at any time. If we love one another, God dwelleth in us, and his love is perfected in us" (I John 4:11,12).

Love is not giving people that which they want when it will ultimately harm them. Love is not giving every word people want to hear. Too many of us say what our friends want to hear because we're cowards and afraid of counterattack.

Well, even in that case, love is standing firm and being kind when people attack us. Besides, we'll get very few counterattacks if we give the truth in love, speaking in a natural way with humility, sweetness and patience.

It's sickening to hear women "coo" to each other about how right and wonderful they are, only to find that later they turn to someone else in criticism of the very one to whom they were "cooing." The Bible says, "Confess your faults one to another, and pray one for another, that ye may be healed. The effectual fervent prayer of a righteous man availeth much" (James 5:16).

In II Timothy 4:2 Paul told Timothy to "exhort with all longsuffering and doctrine." And surely He has given a formula for us to pattern after in dealing with one another.

Too often we let a grievance build in us until we just unload the whole thing in a spirit of anger, never caring whether or not the victim of our wrath is helped. All right, then we see love is sometimes giving words people don't want to hear; love is also giving those words with longsuffering and reason.

There's a Woman in the Church and She Isn't Love

One day my husband was reciting some Scripture as we drove down the highway, and as he recited, "Let nothing be done through strife or vainglory; but in lowliness of mind let each esteem other better than themselves. Look not every man on his own things, but every man also on the things of others" (Phil. 2:3,4), I heard him add, "That would surely take the steam out of any church fuss."

My heart aches as I hear about church problems, because I know, "There is a woman in the church." Maybe she's not "it" openly, but she's there in all her "glory" working somewhere behind the scenes. How often have you heard this or a similar conversation? "Hey, what happened over at church?" "Well, there was this woman in the church." You've said it all!

There's a Woman in the Church and She Is Love

Now, before you accuse me of all kinds of things, let me ask you to think on this point. If a person can think a woman is that important on the negative side, how important does that same person think a woman can be on the positive side?

Oh, wow! That is what I love to talk about, dream of, pray for, write toward and promote in every way possible—that "different" woman whose price is far above rubies and whose tongue speaks with the law of kindness. Proverbs 31:10,26—"Who can find a virtuous woman? for her price is far above rubies. She openeth her mouth with wisdom; and in her tongue is the law of kindness."

That's the kind I long to be—the kind many of you crave to be. Since we say we are not there yet, let's accept one another as we are, exhorting one another and praying for one another as we head toward that goal. Let's have the whole town saying, "Those women at that church are really something. My, how they love each other! You couldn't get one of them to say something bad about another one for anything."

I kind of believe that is what love is, and I've figured out that people will come to see why we love as we do and we can point them to Jesus.

Suppose so? "A new commandment I give unto you, That ye love one another; as I have loved you, that ye also love one another. By this shall all men know that ye are my disciples, if ye have love one to another" (John 13:34,35).

If my thinking is right, I've some tall loving to do. While some folks are easy for me to love, there are others I just don't understand. There are those who are just different from me, and some are plain bad.

I must love:

1. . . . the liar who hardly knows she lies, and the painfully honest one who tortures herself (and me) trying to remember if she told the whole truth and nothing but the truth.

2. . . . the shy, timid introvert who says, "I can't take your time. You're too busy," and the seemingly brash, brazen person who barges in and takes over.

3. . . . the loud, exuberant tomboy who is having real difficulty adjusting to being a Christian lady, and the super-feminine creature who speaks so softly (all in the name of femininity) that she can't be heard.

4. . . . the new convert who doesn't want to be told a thing, and the helpless gal who wants to place her very life in my hands.

5. . . . the girl who is pure because she's fought for purity, and the girl about whom a guy says, "She's easy."

6. . . . the woman who watches her manner of dress and pays the price to be modest, and the woman who says, "I don't think it matters. I'll dress the way I want."

7. . . . the people who wouldn't complain or gripe about anything, and people who gripe and look for things to criticize.

8. . . . those who "waste" no time talking, never laugh and feel all "talk is cheap," and those who try to dominate with meaningless chatter.

9. . . . ladies who give themselves enthusiastically to any project in the Lord's work, and ladies who say, "I don't care to get involved."

Go ahead—make up your own list; add to mine. I could go on and on. As far as I know, there is no perfect group of ladies. Therefore, if you love, you will have to love imperfect human beings—ones you understand and ones you don't; ones who are your type and ones who aren't.

Aren't you glad you don't have to do the loving? The Holy Spirit will love them through you if you let Him. We're only asking for a miracle, and He's in the miracle-working business!

"God is love" (I John 4:8) and His Spirit is in us if we know the Lord Jesus as our Saviour. Therefore, we can be love!

"There is a woman in the church." She spreads joy abroad! She is love! Are you?

7 – The Goal Is Growth

Awhile back I'd been feeling really "icky" for a few days—didn't want to stay in bed, didn't want to go anywhere, didn't want to talk to anyone, didn't want to do anything—at least not anything constructive. I will say this for me, though: I did some thinking. Some of it was good, too! Let me share some of my thoughts with you.

Babies—Never!

On January 29, 1963, the adoption agency called to ask if we wanted to come see a baby girl. So January 30 I left nine other little "babies" I had taught for a year and a half. My thoughts during those days in bed centered on those nine kids I left those many years ago. They surely wouldn't want to be called "babies," for they were never babies. They had experienced more in their six, seven or eight years of life than many of us will ever experience in a whole lifetime. They worked so hard for every little fraction of an inch of growth and were so thrilled to see a tiny bit of improvement. You see, they were orthopedically handicapped children.

I loved to see them grow. Their growth made me think of Matthew 13:32: "Which indeed is the least of all seeds: but when it is grown, it is the greatest among herbs, and becometh a tree, so that the birds of the air come and lodge in the branches thereof."

Darlin' Debbie

A little girl I called "Darlin' Debbie" would come dancing in with her whole body in uncontrollable motion, fling the top of her head toward me and say, "See my stitches; I fell again." She soon had to add a football helmet to her otherwise immaculate and very feminine ensembles.

The floor of our schoolroom was made of 3″-wide boards, and we worked and worked trying to help Debbie come straight to the front of the room down one of the 3″-boards. I'd say, "Come straight down the board to me, Deb." When she grew in ability to walk straight toward me, we clapped and cheered, which excited her to the point that she'd lose her balance again. We'd all laugh and have a good time, but I'd think, *How hard it is to grow!*

A Butterball Topped With White Ringlets

Roger, that fat little blue-eyed butterball topped with white ringlets, spent a good part of the day asking about a second roll at lunch. Every child could have a second roll if the first roll was eaten. Roger's head and arms flew back and forth most of the time, and they really went into action when he was anxious about anything. Therefore, he'd bob head and arms at me wildly asking, "Do I get a second roll? Do I get a second roll? Do I get a second roll?" just as fast as he could spit out the words. My calm, supposedly reassuring words, "Roger, eat the roll you have first; then you'll get another one," didn't seem to penetrate—not for very long anyway. It was the same every day as well as I can remember.

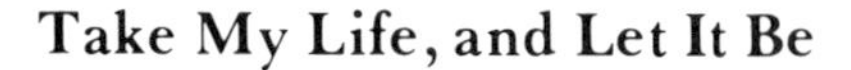

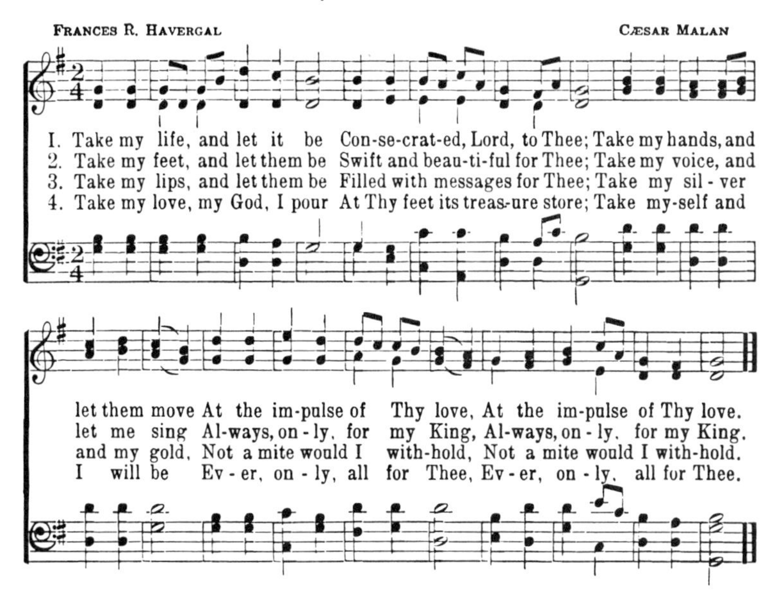

Our Goal: Growth

Every word of each of the songs we've used in connection with *Christian Womanhood* has to do with goals for growth in the Lord. I really believe most of us want to grow. Then, why is it that we grow so little? We use all kinds of reasoning to excuse ourselves: "We have only a few weeks of school left. I'll let down." Yes, and you'll fail! "I'm at the end of my life. I don't need to grow now." Yes, and you'll die prematurely, too!

I wonder if all these excuses boil down to being lazy, proud or ignorant.

Is It Laziness?

For those orthopedically handicapped "young 'uns," growth meant being locked into the notch of a standing table in order to develop strength and stability. It meant big, heavy neck collars to control involuntary head movement. It meant balancing bars, braces, exercises and therapy ad nauseam. It wasn't fun to grow. The fun came after the growth.

Recently I read a book which pointed out the fact that "training means growing and growing means stretching. Growing is not a pleasant experience."

Remember how your child hurt when he began to learn to walk? When he fell you said, "I know it hurts. Get up and go again."

Remember the mixed emotions of growing into womanhood? You wanted to become a woman, and you didn't want to become a woman. It hurts to grow.

"Growing is so painful that the first chance we get we want to stop. Our desire to escape the pain of growth is so great an obstacle to overcome. We begin to coast on past experiences. Having begun well, we drift into mediocrity."

That quote perfectly describes my piano lessons. I had "Here We Go Up the Road to a Birthday Party" pretty well mastered. And then that piano teacher wanted me to try something harder. I messed up on "the something harder." I could play "Here We Go . . ." without mistakes and didn't have to work over and over on certain sections of it. I knew it and enjoyed showing how well I knew it. I can still show how well I know it. (That's the only song I can show how well I know.) I didn't want criticism. I didn't want help. I banged the piano keys and said, "I don't want to play an old piano anyway." Guess what? I can't! I got my way. It was too hard to grow. Was I lazy?

Is It Pride?

Why don't we grow? Is false pride the answer?

Have you ever asked a friend to give you constructive criticism? You said, "If you see anything in me that bothers you, please tell me. I want all the help I can get."

Then when the day came when that help was given, you found yourself making excuses and giving explanations for that which had been pointed out to you. Of course, the friend realizes you don't really want help, and she does not offer it again. In fact, she'll probably return to the usual habit of giving you soothing sympathy which is poison to growth.

Growth is stopped by negative statements (excuses) such as these: "I'm only human," "I'm already better than I used to be," "I know some people who are worse than I am," "That's just not my strength," "I'm just that way," and, "You can't expect me to be perfect."

No, we are not going to be perfect as Jesus our Saviour is perfect, but we can mature on our way toward the goal He has set for us. "Be ye therefore perfect, even as your Father which is in heaven is perfect" (Matt. 5:48). We can develop in mature godliness and kindness.

I've often heard my husband preach about growth being a command and not a suggestion. A good Christian has no choice but to grow. "But grow in grace, and in the knowledge of our Lord and Saviour Jesus Christ. To him be glory both now and for ever. Amen" (II Pet. 3:18).

Jesus grew, and He is the very Son of God. "And Jesus increased in wisdom [mental] and stature [physical], and in favour with God [spiritual] and man [social]" (Luke 2:52).

Yes, pride keeps us from growing! We won't go near an experience in which we don't feel competent because we're afraid to admit to ourselves or to anyone else that there's something we don't know.

We're all immature in some areas, and it hurts to admit it. However, hurt is going to come through that area whether or not we grow within it. The hurt will be greatly lessened if we admit the weakness and get help rather than coddle and nurse the fault while attempting to hide it.

Is It Ignorance?

Do we fail to grow because we keep ourselves in ignorance about our need for growth?

Throughout my years of teaching I've always been concerned about the students (of any age) who busy themselves in an excess amount of work at which they're expert. I was afraid that a student who studied and did extra work for the school to the point that she never had time for activities or friends was hiding from the fact that she had not developed normally in the field of human relations.

On the other hand, a student who always has time for activities and friends seems to set herself up to be able to say, "I just don't have time to study." Maybe this person doesn't even know what she's doing.

As a Christian leader, it's all too easy to allow a person to stunt her growth by sapping all her strength in the one area in which she is good. If we really care about people, we will encourage them to develop into a complete person even if it means losing some help for awhile.

Christian lady, how would you apply this student example to your life? Is it possible that you've involved yourself outside the home to such a great extent that you really don't have time for the home and family? Did the Lord really direct you to get that busy, or are you keeping yourself in ignorance about the fact that you don't feel competent in the home?

Mrs. Homemaker, when you always say, "I can't go soul winning; I'm too busy at home," are you playing games to help you remain ignorant about your need to learn to win souls?

Come Straight Down the Board and Don't Ask for the Second Roll!

"Come straight down the board to me, Deb." Jesus is saying, "Come straight down the board to Me, Lady! Here's my goal for you: GROW!" "As newborn babes, desire the sincere milk of the word, that ye may grow thereby: If so be ye have tasted that the Lord is gracious" (I Pet. 2:2,3).

Take the step of growth God has for you right now. Don't ask, "Do I get a second roll? Do I get a second roll?" Finish the task that God has for you now!

8 – The Reason and the Requirement

Why do we want to be used? Why are we here? What is our reason for living?

There is really only one reason, and that is to reproduce. To reproduce spiritually is to have children and grandchildren, yes, great and even great-great-grandchildren in the Lord. In that way we repay those who reproduced themselves in us. Yes, we will die if we do not reproduce!

Today there's so much emphasis placed on reproducing physically and a great deal of talk concerning the "empty-nest syndrome"—a time in the life of a woman when she feels she is no longer needed by her children and, therefore, feels dull, useless and unwanted.

The women's magazines are full of stories about forty-and forty-five-year-old women who pull up in front of doctors' offices in beautiful cars. They have just left luxurious houses and are decked out in the latest fashions. Seemingly they have everything for which to live. Yet they are discontented to the point that they're visiting doctor after doctor with no real physical complaint. They are sick! They are dying! It's all because they are no longer reproducing themselves in the lives of someone else. If the doctor would write a prescription with "Jesus and Others" on it, the "disease" would be cured.

Perhaps you've never had children in your home. Maybe you are a single lady or a married woman who has never mothered children. You must avoid that "empty-nest syndrome." That empty nest can begin very early in life if you fail to reproduce spiritually. Reproducing is the only way to keep living.

It's a beautiful chain reaction. Just throw a pebble into the lake and watch the ripples until you can no longer see them. It's casting your bread upon waters. It's action! It's life! It's excitement! It's living life to its very fullest! It's the abundant life! John 10:10 says, "I am come that they might have life, and that they might have it more abundantly."

If your reason for living is to reproduce, words will come out of you which you didn't know you knew. Ideas will spring from your mind as if you were a fountain of wisdom. You will be able to do things you didn't know you knew how to do. All because you allow the Holy Spirit to work in you in order to reach others.

Give yourself in three ways—give in, give up and give out! Give in to the Holy Spirit's conviction which tells you to live for others. Give up your way for God's way in your life, saying, "I surrender all." When you give up to Him you really surrender your will in complete obedience to His. Then, give out to everyone around you. That's the only way to keep living. You either reproduce or die.

You reproduce by planting a seed (as a mustard seed) and sometimes you wonder when you're ever going to reap a harvest. So many times I've found that when I thought I did something, I had done nothing; and when I thought I'd done nothing, I had done something. That's because I didn't do it in the first place; the Lord Jesus did it through me.

I'm sure some of the following stories (which remind me that I do not know when I do or do not do anything) have come back to me for a reason. God wants to help me recall the fact that it is always He who does anything that I'm allowed to see happen. None of us are of the wise.

"For ye see your calling, brethren, how that not many wise men after the flesh, not many mighty, not many noble, are called: But God hath chosen the foolish things of the world to confound the wise; and God hath chosen the weak things of the world to confound the things which are mighty; And base things of the world, and things which are despised, hath God chosen, yea, and things which are not, to bring to nought things that are" (I Cor. 1:26-28).

When my husband was in graduate school at Bob Jones University, we had the opportunity to work in a church in Asheville, North Carolina, on weekends. It was quite a drive from Greenville, South Carolina, to Asheville every weekend in that old '49 Plymouth, which had bald tires and holes in the floor through which water sloshed. We didn't know that we really did much during the few months we traveled back and forth through the mountains, but we felt that we had received valuable experience for later work.

A number of years after that experience, we happened to visit Bob Jones University and ran into a young lady who had been a recent graduate of the school. She came running up to us and said, "Remember me?" We did, for we had stayed in the home of her parents quite a few weekends during the time we traveled back and forth to Asheville those months. She told us that she was now teaching part-time at Bob Jones while her husband was receiving his training to be a pastor. She explained their plans for starting a local church one day soon.

I said, "Carol, how did you happen to come to Bob Jones University?" She said, "Don't you remember when you used to come and talk to me about the school when you stayed at our home?" She had been in the seventh grade that year! We had talked to scores of people who were in the eleventh or twelfth grades and were actual candidates for college. Yet, God chose to work in His own way helping that one girl to remember what we had said while she was in the seventh grade. It seemed as if He was saying, "Remember, I'm the One who does the work!"

First Corinthians 3:5-7 reminds us of this also:

"Who then is Paul, and who is Apollos, but ministers by whom ye believed, even as the Lord gave to every man? I have planted, Apollos watered; but God gave the increase. So then neither is he that planteth any thing, neither he that watereth; but God that giveth the increase."

One day my husband received a letter from Dr. Vineyard, who was our church bus director, in which he let us know that he had met a bus captain on a Ft. Riley, Kansas, bus route who had been one of our bus kids back in Ringgold, Georgia. I got word about the letter without knowing the name of the person involved.

I thought and thought. What kid from our bus route had become a bus captain—with sixty on his route? I thought of John, but no. . . the first few months on our route he had been a help; but the last year we had with him was a catastrophe. He always dragged on the bus and headed toward the rear with defiance and rebellion written all over his face. But you know what! Yes, you guessed it; he is the one!

It's no use to try to figure out what you do and what you don't do. The Lord does it all anyway, and He will tell each of us what happened for sure when we get to the place where the records are kept. Let's just keep on reproducing for His glory!

The reason for living is to reproduce. We reproduce by winning souls and building in the lives of those around us. One reason for living is to keep from dying! I have decided that we'll never have to die if we invest our lives in those around us. We'll spend eternity in Heaven and go on living on earth until Jesus comes the second time! According to Revelation 14:13 our works do follow after us: "And I heard a voice from heaven saying unto me, Write, Blessed are the dead which die in the Lord from henceforth: Yea, saith the Spirit, that they may rest from their labours; and their works do follow them." They just go on and on.

I like to live, don't you? I think it's just great that God gave us a plan by which we can live in Heaven and on earth at the same time.

The Requirements

Education? Good looks? Great talent? None of these is the answer to being used of God. No, these are not the requirements. Good looks can be a blessing if used for God, but usually they are a curse. Society seems to reward pretty little girls and handsome young boys just for being good-looking. This is a terrible thing, because a child who grows up under this doesn't have to work or learn to be pleasant to people to make it in this world.

I've often heard teachers say, "He's so cute. I just can't say no to him!" or, "She looked at me with those sparkling brown eyes, and I melted!"

Good looks may ruin you. Every person is basically a giving or receiving person. The very attractive person has to fight the temptation to give in to those who would make her just a receiving person in order to have the privilege of her company. Laban's daughters, Rachel and Leah, are good examples of the giving and the receiving person. It's wonderful to know that God can use both, as He did in their case. However, good looks certainly aren't the answer to being used of God.

Is it talent? No! One time Dr. Bob Jones, Sr., told us about a lovely girl who had come to school with an expensive violin. She spent most of her time practicing that violin. It meant more to her than anything—it really meant more to her than the Lord Jesus and doing His work. Dr. Bob asked her to give him the violin until she was able to put it in its proper place. He locked it in a safe and kept it until the day she felt that she could really use the violin for God.

I remember a little girl back in my home town. She was so sweet that when my mother said to my sister, "Doris, why don't you play with her?" Doris answered, "Mama, she's just too nice a girl for me to play with." That's always been one of our family jokes because we thought Doris was a pretty good girl, but we weren't quite sure about her after that remark!

When I was sixteen years old I had a little junior choir, and Doris' friend was one of the girls in that choir. By that time she was on her way to becoming a concert pianist. She was really good, so good that when she graduated from high school and went on into her work, she received parts in movies as a pianist and had concerts in European countries.

Her talent gave her temptations she would never have had without it. One time a sensational magazine published a picture of her which made my heart ache as I thought of the sweet young girl Doris thought was too nice.

Talent can be used, but it is not the answer to your being used. If not controlled, it can be a curse.

Education can be used for God, but education without Christ is not the answer. Dr. Bob Jones, Sr., used to say, "The criminal who forged checks first had to learn to write." He also said, "I'd rather have a man who says, 'I seen,' who has really seen something, than one who says, 'I have seen' when he hasn't seen anything!" That great man also said, "I'd rather have a little cabin mother who hasn't finished grade school but can tell me about Jesus, than a mother with a Ph.D. who doesn't know Him."

For sure, three words which might be the answer to being used of God are "die, want and give." Die to your sins and your wants. Want for God and for others. Wanting more for others than you do for yourself will help you to be used for others; and yes, it might even be a requirement for being used of God. Yes, give up, give in and give out!

A requirement to being used is to learn from each other and admit it. Glory in the knowledge and victories of one another. Die to jealousy.

Dying, wanting and giving have to do with glorifying God.

"What? know ye not that your body is the temple of the Holy Ghost which is in you, which ye have of God, and ye are not your own? For ye are bought with a price: therefore glorify God in your body, and in your spirit, which are God's" (I Cor. 6:19,20).

The requirements call for us to do all for the glory of God. "Whether therefore ye eat, or drink, or whatsoever ye do, do all to the glory of God" (I Cor. 10:31).

We must be willing to be last. If we put ourselves last, He will put us first. If we put ourselves down, He will put us up.

Recently I read some words that were a great help to me:

"The key to living is dying; the key to being free is being Christlike; the key to getting is giving; the key to being a leader is being a servant. The key to being exalted is living a life of humility."

"Everybody wants to live, but nobody wants to die. Everybody wants to be free, but nobody wants to be a slave. Everybody wants to get, but nobody wants to give."

No, lady, you don't have to have good looks, talent or education. You have to love—which is to die, to want and to give. If you help women, someone will drop them through the roof to you. They'll find a way to get to you. You won't have to worry about finding them. You just love.

All the requirements kind of boil down to giving up, giving in and giving out!

9 – The Result and the Reward

The Result

If you have accepted spiritual reproduction as the goal for your life—yes, even your very reason for living—if you have paid the price by meeting the requirements, you will see some results.

You'll be endowed with a supernatural power to do a supernatural job. None of us is worthy of spiritual reproduction. If it is done, God has to do it through us. You will no longer live a normal life. Yes, you'll be considered slightly abnormal.

Now don't do anything to try to be a little different. You'll be different enough as you live New Testament love and Christianity. Being different isn't your goal; it's the natural result of your goal. Folks will whisper the adjectives, "strange," "peculiar," "different," "fanatical," in connection with your name. You'll even seem a bit strange to yourself.

As you become consumed with a completely different reason for living, you will do things that make you say to yourself, *This is ridiculous!*

One time I served with bus workers who gathered at what seemed an unearthly hour to check their buses and get ready to be abused. Some of them actually knew they were facing situations which would cause them heartache. They got up early on the only morning they could sleep late to start old buses that refused to go in order to pick up people who wouldn't come. This has to be strange—or is it a miracle in the heart of a sinner saved by grace?

The result of having spiritual reproduction as a goal and the result of paying the price to reach that goal is a BROKEN HEART.

Sometimes a girl comes to me wanting to know how she can really care about her bus kids. I think of churches that say, "People can get there if they want to badly enough." (The only thing is, they won't.) "Let the church that's near their house get them. We don't believe in this running all over the country." (The only thing is, no one goes.)

Then the girl and I pray: "Lord, most churches won't get them and don't help them. Parents won't bring them. Help us to love them when no one else does."

Then I ask the girl to take her Bible and go off by herself, to walk and cry as she asks God to break her heart over her kids, just as Christ's heart was broken over her. I recommend that she read the crucifixion chapters over and over, absorbing the fanatical, strange, abnormal and peculiar thing Christ did for her.

When I taught special children, I learned that I could buy a certain amount of "expendable" materials from Title I government funds. After much discussion, I determined which orders I could classify "expendable." These are things which could be spent or used completely with no remains, such as paper clips, paper, crayons and anything else which would not remain in the classroom year after year. Globes and maps were non-expendables.

I want to be "expendable" in the most exciting cause the world has ever known—REPRODUCING FOR THE CAUSE OF CHRIST! I want to be used completely! I want the girl to love her bus kids and spend herself completely as Christ spent Himself for her.

Telling you the results of reproducing and paying the price—telling you that you might be misunderstood—is a little sad, but the story doesn't end here. Read on!

The Reward

"Cast thy bread upon the waters: for thou shalt find it after many days" (Eccles. 11:1).

Farmers in Nebraska interested me when I was a kid. They wanted to produce crops. They plowed, planted, irrigated, weeded, sprayed and paid a tremendous price. They were a wee bit weird in how they were consumed. Their eyes were always toward the heavens as they watched for rain or storms.

I never thought I'd like all that control over my reason for living. I didn't think I wanted to meet the requirements they seemed to think they had to meet. I didn't like the results of the whole thing. They could talk of nothing but crops. Weather was the big news of the day.

However, I really could take to that harvest time! My dad worked as a foreman at a flour mill, and I'd go watch him supervise the unloading of trucks of wheat. Sometimes as many as sixteen trucks would be in line to be weighed and unloaded. It was a beautiful sight!

At times we'd take a ride late at night to see lights of twenty combines criss-crossing the flat lands as they gathered in the harvest. What excitement, drama and challenge! Yes, I've always loved the harvest!

Once when my husband spoke in Aledo, Illinois, our family got to stay with the late Art and Emma Tompkins in their log cabin along the Mississippi River. Art told me he put 200 fish hooks in the water. Some mornings he had a great big harvest; other times it was small. He would go out in the rain to run his lines. He kept wondering how many fish he had; he couldn't wait to go see. He was consumed by a cause, and he appeared a little strange over his cause.

What makes a man go out in the rain at 6:00 a.m. before breakfast? A harvest!

When I was eleven and twelve years old, I picked strawberries, tomatoes and cucumbers in "Boo" Boughen's truck garden in Blue Springs, Nebraska. A few mornings I asked Dad to get me up at 4:00 a.m. in order to have time to ride my bicycle to the garden. Sometimes where there was still more to be gathered as a storm came up, "Boo" would tell us, "Quit your broadcasting" (talking) "and stay out in that patch until the harvest is in." Wild looks came into our eyes as we raced down the rows to save the harvest from sure destruction.

The first year I was away from home, my mother had a serious operation, and I wrote my dad of my love and support of him, especially during that time. I told him I was sorry for the trouble I'd caused in my growing-up years. He answered with these words: "We weren't looking at the day-by-day picture but for the end result."

I guess parents look for a harvest way down at the end of the row someplace. I've thought of that statement one million times as I've been led of God to work with college students almost twenty-five years. So often I've been tempted just to mark "zero" on a student! When I just about decide she will never be anything, that statement comes back to me saying, "Marlene, you'd better wait before you toss her out as hopeless. Look for the end result. Maybe you'll get a good harvest this time."

It's worth a wild-eyed look as you race down the row of a girl's life to try to bring in the harvest before she's ruined!

Who knows what's big and what's little? I've always been so confused by what person is big and what person is little. Just as soon as I've thought someone was big, it turned out she wasn't. Then when I've thought someone was little, she turned out to be big.

People, in light of this, all I know to do is to plan to treat everybody as if she is big. You can't miss that way. Let's give cups of cold water in His name to everyone. I believe the Lord wants us to be confused. He likes to surprise us about what we've done when we thought we did nothing, and what we haven't done when we thought we did something. I also think He likes to see our reactions when we find out who is big when we thought they were little.

Oh, the harvest time! I can still see the waving fields of golden grain being invaded by the combines as they went in for the reward.

Look at I Corinthians. Read all of chapter 3. Verse 14 says, "If any man's work abide which he hath built thereupon, he shall receive a reward."

Is it worth it? Ten thousand times over! If your reason for living is to reproduce spiritually, you'll have to meet some tough requirements. Some results you won't like. People won't understand you. But my, oh my, the reward is just. . . I don't know how to tell you how wonderful it is!

I know! As you began to reproduce in physical life, didn't you have to go through some tough requirements in order to keep that unborn baby healthy? Didn't you pay the price? Then, what were the results of paying that price? Did you seem a bit strange? Was your mind consumed with caring for that unborn baby?

Now, remember the reward? Remember that feeling when that warm little baby was placed in your arms—perfect and healthy? That's the harvest!

When I see a girl's life change from one of bitterness, rebellion and hatred to one of submission in all sweetness to God and human authority, I feel as you must have felt when God placed your baby in your arms.

Several years ago a girl came to Hyles-Anderson College with more open rebellion and hostility than should be able to happen in a lifetime. The bitterness and hatefulness almost floored me.

One dear older lady, loved by all the students, sweetly asked my girl, "What's your name, honey?" to which the girl snapped,

"What do you want to know for?" The student let me know shortly that she didn't trust me or anyone else.

Some people thought I was strange to let her talk to me as I did. A few whispered about their sorrow for me since they could see that I didn't "have the picture" on that girl. They no doubt suspected premature senility on my part. I don't mean I let her get by with things I should have reported to my authorities, but you who work with kids know what you put up with sometimes while you're waiting for the harvest.

Let me share some words from recent notes from her:

> Please pray for me, Mrs. Evans. The verses in Romans 7:18, 19 have been so true of me. Why won't people learn the first time? Everything you said I was, I am. I love you so much for seeing it and telling me. I wish I had been strong enough to take it. I guess the truth always hurts. I can see now how ugly I've been toward you. I am so sorry!
>
> * * *
>
> The first time I saw you, or remember seeing you, was the day after I received a note in my mailbox. It said, "See me in my office tomorrow." I began checking you out! Just who was Mrs. Evans? I was eighteen and thought that was pretty old!
>
> If I remember correctly, I couldn't wait to get out of your office. I was rude and acted ugly. I thought for sure you really wanted to get me kicked out or something!
>
> Since then, you have gone through my terrible temper series—loud, noisy outbursts, uncontrollable sense of reasoning, the mini-bike escapade and hospital stay, other childish pranks, and mistrust of everything and everyone.
>
> I guess I haven't gotten rid of it all yet, but I know what to pray about and work on in hopes of having a well-balanced Christian life. I guess I've learned a lot in the years of classes, talks, phone calls, notes and letters.

The harvest is beginning to come in! I plan to reap from now through eternity. Oh, the harvest time!

10 – Love Is Teamwork

One time my husband and I went to the University of Tennessee to see Tennessee and Auburn play. If you've ever seen them play, you know that it was some game! That year Bill Battle was the coach. It was his first year, and he was the youngest major college coach in the nation.

I don't know anything about football, and I don't think you know any more about it than I do. There are some posts down at the end of the field. (It is a field, isn't it?) Yes, there are some posts at the end or something, and people get all excited if the person has the ball. That's about all I know.

I Was a "Scout" at a U.T. Game!

There were 40,000 fans there, and I was taking notes. I ruined the whole game for the man beside me because I write so terribly. He couldn't read my notes written on tiny little pieces of scrap paper. I'm sure he thought I was a scout. Who else would sit at a football game and take notes like that?

But as I saw what was happening on that football field, I thought, *Wow! This is something that should be happening in a home. This is something that should be happening in a Sunday school class or a Christian college or a church. Love is teamwork!*

First Corinthians 12 Teaches Football!

Let's look at I Corinthians 12:12-17 for a little while.

"For as the body is one, and hath many members, and all the members of that one body, being many, are one body: so also is Christ. For by one Spirit are we all baptized into one body, whether we be Jews or Gentiles, whether we be bond or free; and have been all made to drink into one Spirit. For the body is not one member, but many. If the foot shall say, Because I am not the hand, I am not of the body; is it therefore not of the body? And if the ear shall say, Because I am not the eye, I am not of the body; is it therefore not of the body? If the whole body were an eye, where were the hearing? If the whole were hearing, where were the smelling?"

Can you imagine one great big eye coming down the street? You'd say, "Is that it?" Yes, that's the whole body. It sounds stupid, but that is exactly what a lot of us would like to see when we don't understand why someone has to be different from us. It's the same thing, isn't it?

In women's groups we want everyone to be the same. But that would be just as gruesome as if a great big eye were coming down the street. We need the whole body.

"If the whole body were an eye, where were the hearing? If the whole were hearing, where were the smelling? But now hath God set the members every one of them in the body, as it hath pleased him. And if they were all one member, where were the body? But now are they many members, yet but one body. And the eye cannot say unto the hand, I have no need of thee: nor again the head to the feet, I have no need of you. Nay, much more those members of the body, which seem to be more feeble, are necessary: And those members of the body, which we think to be less honourable, upon these we bestow more abundant honour; and our uncomely parts have more abundant comeliness. For our comely parts have no need: but God hath tempered the body together, having given more abundant honour to that part which lacked: That there should be no schism in the body; but that the members should have the same care one for another. And whether one member suffer, all the members suffer with it; or one member be honoured, all the members rejoice with it" (I Cor. 12:17-26).

Yes, we suffer together! As I came to our college one morning, I stopped to talk to Linda Shogren, who was our nurse at the time. She said, "My brother and two nephews drowned last night." I thought, *This is the time for the body to come together. Linda Shogren is our nurse! She has helped us; she's been with us when we've been sick, and now it is our turn to gather around her. We can get her airline tickets, take her to the airport, see that she has something to eat, and be certain she is taken care of until she leaves to go home. This is the time.*

I have seen the time when one of my sisters in Christ did something terribly wrong. That was my time to say, *The body is hurting; I must rush to the rescue and help.* That was not the time to say, *I have no need of thee,* or, *I'll have nothing to do with you.* We may have to talk firmly as we give Scripture. Love will have to be given in its purest form—which may include scolding and discipline. That's sometimes exactly what the member of the body needs.

First Corinthians 12 ends with, "But covet earnestly the best gifts: and yet shew I unto you a more excellent way." Then God proceeds to tell us of that great love in I Corinthians 13 which is more excellent than all the preceding gifts being discussed.

We are one body in Christ and should always be ready to help one another. Part of this principle is known by a winning football team.

A Whole New Team for Each Different Play!

You cannot believe how readily those guys came running to the bench when a new team went onto the field. They would start a new thing going (something about offensive and defensive); and the coach would call some off the field. I didn't see any of them say anything. They just came out, sat down and shut up!

Oh, if we could do that as women used of God. . .just fade out when we're not needed, sit down and shut up! If those big men will do that for the cause of a football game, then why won't we do it for the cause of Christ in our churches and homes? What could be done if we sometimes would shut up!!! Sometimes I say to myself, "Shut Up!" "Keep Still!" "Be Quiet!" or "Hush!" but this doesn't always work.

The question is not whether you are used the way you want to be used or not, but whether you are being used the way God wants to use you!

They Made Space for the One Being Used!

Some of you ladies and girls know exactly what this means because you've sometimes been the one to see that a place was made for the one being used. You didn't receive the honor, and no one jumped up and yelled your name; but you've seen to it that the one carrying the ball reached the goal. If all of us would do that in churches, it would be pretty difficult for the devil to stop us.

I remember an incident when a pastor's wife came to me and said, "I don't dare take this program home because that assistant pastor's wife would jump up to do it, taking right over."

I said, "Could she do it?"

The lady said, "Well, yes."

I said, "Is there any reason she shouldn't do it?"

"No."

"Then why don't you take this program to her, telling her she is the very one to do it and that you'll back her and pray for her, making a way for her."

"Ohhhhhh," she said.

I remember a little church in which the pastor had to walk

to the pulpit through the center aisle. You could see a certain woman getting ready as if she thought this was the time to tell him everything she had heard. "Oh, Pastor, let me tell you this," she would say, just as he walked up to preach the sermon. I think this is an opponent tackling the one running with the ball.

Could you run up and tackle the opponent? (I don't mean physically!) No, let's be nice. Jump up and say, "Come sit with me. That's a pretty dress. Did you make it?"

Now you should also get ready to be attacked yourself! Almost any time you are doing something for God, someone will want to deflate you. People just love to put a pin in your balloon. They might not know what they are doing! Sometimes they do. They are reacting against the fact that you are excited! They aren't doing anything, so they have to find a way to bring you to their level.

If you allow them to do it, you've really let them hurt you. Here's a better way. Get them involved with you in God's work. The noise in the apartment upstairs doesn't seem so loud after you are invited to the party. Know what I mean?

I have people who tackle opponents for me. I can hear you say, "Isn't that humiliating for them?" I think the rewards for anything God lets me do belong mostly to these people. Humiliating? Nothing is humiliating if it's for the cause of Christ and the body. Being a foot is not humiliating. I know that is not the most lovely or beautiful part of the body in the world's eyes, but being a foot is not humiliating when the foot is being used for the Lord Jesus Christ.

Some of these people don't have to be "tackles." Although most of these who tackle opponents for me could be anything they wanted to be in their own rights, God has chosen them to tackle opponents for others.

I've tried to be that to some other people. Sometimes we can do that for someone and someone else can do that for us. What a beautiful picture of the body of Christ working together, with Jesus Christ as the Head!

Look at your hands! Despite what you think, they are beautiful! Those fingers and that thumb are miraculous machines. He gave us that hand so it could be used for the Lord Jesus Christ. The wrist can turn. When all that is in that wrist begins deteriorating and grinding together to shoot out pain, it's unbelievable how little you're able to do with your hand. The doctor says, "Come to the hospital where we'll open up that wrist and fuse some bones together so you'll not have the pain anymore." Afterwards, you are not able to turn your hands as well, and you have to use both hands to support any small weight.

Whether it is a part of the physical body or a part of the body of Christ, we don't appreciate it until it's gone. I think we ought to make a lot over our husbands and all members of the body of Christ while they are alive. Let's encourage them by tackling their opponents today. Let's encourage them now!

We're so embarrassed to go up to a member of the body and say, "I love you." We're not embarrassed to gossip about them, but we are embarrassed to tell them we love them. Just now I am slapping my own face. If you were to see me slapping my own face, you would say, "What's the matter with you?" Yet, that's what you are doing when you talk about someone who is a part of the body of Christ. It's that ridiculous!

There Were Back-Up People Who Warmed Benches!

I understand that they fly those bench-warmers across the country to warm benches. They say the coach and team need to know the bench-warmers are there. I mean they spend thousands of dollars to fly men around the country who don't play at all!

There are some people in churches who are seldom used. Very few times do they do anything that is really seen, but they are there all the time—which encourages others. If you are a bench-warmer, or if you feel as if you are a bench-warmer, spend that extra time you have praying and willing your strength and smile to the one being used.

There have been times in my life when God has set me aside and let me be a bench-warmer. During those times I've tried to say to others, "You can do it! You can do it! I know you can!" I thank God for those times, for I believe they were used to show me that I ought to help other people be used.

The ball players don't have a choice about being on the bench. Sometimes we do. So many times we say, "I'd rather do it myself! If I don't do it myself, it won't be done right." Instead, let's say, "I want to see some others do the job. I'm willing to sacrifice having it done exactly the way that I want it, in order to allow someone else to develop and have the joy of doing God's work."

Now sometimes this is a big headache because we leave out a little word of the "organize, deputize, supervise" syndrome. Some really tragic things happen when we leave out supervision. You don't have to "snoopervise," but you do need to say, "Can I help you with this project? Let me check back with you." Then do exactly that!

We become so anxious that sometimes we jump in and take over. I know all those temptations, and you do, too. Some of us have done that with our children until they don't want to do anything. Let's teach and supervise so this won't happen. Have you done this with your husband?

I once was talking with a couple, and as I directed questions the husband's way, I heard the answers coming from the little lady by his side. For awhile I thought I had a case of ventriloquism on my hands. Really, I think the lady became ill at ease and was afraid to wait for her husband to take the time to form the words for his own answers. False pride plays a big part in this type of thing, don't you think?

"If I ask someone else, she will think I don't want to do it, that I'm just lazy!" is an excuse for not sharing God's work. That's not the thing at all! We're members in a body. We all work together—players and bench-warmers—with Christ as the Head. As we work as a team, backing each one as we find different things people can do, it's going to be difficult for the devil to stop us.

A Band and Cheerleaders

A band and cheerleaders really had all kinds of things happening. They came out at half time. That's the part of the game I understood. The band performed in beautiful formations, and cheerleaders came out to direct the turning of the pompons different ways, with lots of spirit and color. I saw nice ladies (who didn't look the part) stand and yell, "ALL THE WAY, BIG TEAM, ALL THE WAY!!!"

That should be our attitude at home—"I'm praying for you; I'm behind you all the way." We ought to quit questioning our husband constantly with "Did you do this?" "Did you do that?" "Do you think you will be able?" The cheerleaders weren't questioning their team; they just kept saying, "All the way! I'm with you!"

I understand that the type of questioning described above can absolutely paralyze a football team. It can also paralyze a family member. Athletes have told me that booing from hecklers can at times get to them.

I'm afraid that sometimes we are hecklers to other members of our church and family. Our whole problem is that we are so smart, we are dumb! We don't seem to know a thing about the fact that LOVE IS TEAMWORK!

If you see you've been failing, remember that love gets hit and gets up again. Get up and begin proving that LOVE IS TEAMWORK!!

11 — Different Women Are Peculiar

Christian Womanhood was founded in May, 1975. It began with a cry for different women; and it's still "same song. . . second verse." Has the "line upon line, precept upon precept" made an impact at all? If it has, you are seeking some rather strange goals for your life. No, on second thought, they're more than strange. . .they are positively weird in today's world!

Death!

While the world is crying, "I want to live," we, along with Paul, really want to mean, "For to me to live is Christ, and to die is gain," and, "I die daily," and, "For thy sake we are killed all the day long; we are accounted as sheep for the slaughter" (Phil. 1:21; I Cor. 15:31; Rom. 8:36).

Mrs. Jack Hyles, truly a different woman, gives testimony to the fact that she had been a pastor's wife many years and had won souls and taught Sunday school before she really GAVE her life to Christ. This we can surely understand since so many of us claim Christ as Saviour but continue to control our own lives.

Mrs. Hyles goes on to tell of a time when she was flying to Texas to visit her mother and said, "Lord, kill me!" She says,

"I didn't mean that I wanted that plane to go down, but that I wanted to die to Beverly Hyles."

Dying to self is not common because we don't die easily. Abandonment of self brings such exciting living that I thought you might want to study these Scriptures:

Joshua 1:8—"This book of the law shall not depart out of thy mouth; but thou shalt meditate therein day and night, that thou mayest observe to do according to all that is written therein: for then thou shalt make thy way prosperous, and then thou shalt have good success."

Romans 12:1, 2—"I beseech you therefore, brethren, by the mercies of God, that ye present your bodies a living sacrifice, holy, acceptable unto God, which is your reasonable service. And be not conformed to this world: but be ye transformed by the renewing of your mind, that ye may prove what is that good, and acceptable, and perfect, will of God."

First Corinthians 9:27—"But I keep under my body, and bring it into subjection: lest that by any means, when I have preached to others, I myself should be a castaway."

First Corinthians 15:31—"I protest by your rejoicing which I have in Christ Jesus our Lord, I die daily."

Galatians 2:20—"I am crucified with Christ: nevertheless I live; yet not I, but Christ liveth in me: and the life which I now live in the flesh I live by the faith of the Son of God, who loved me, and gave himself for me."

Second Timothy 2:3,4,11—"Thou therefore endure hardness, as a good soldier of Jesus Christ. No man that warreth entangleth himself with the affairs of this life; that he may please him who hath chosen him to be a soldier. It is a faithful saying: For if we be dead with him, we shall also live with him."

Yes, I know the world says, "I want to live." However, those who die are the only ones who can really live! "He that findeth his life shall lose it: and he that loseth his life for my sake shall find it" (Matt. 10:39).

We live in direct proportion to the degree to which we have died! In fact, death to self is a prerequisite to all other goals we seek.

Bondage!

We, as different women, seek to be bondservants to the Lord Jesus Christ as we give up all claim to our own lives. No wonder the world says, "Strange," "different," "peculiar," and yes, "weird." We need to be kind and gentle at every opportunity in order to soften the blow because if we're truly different, we're too much of a shock to the world.

As the women of the world cry, "I want to be free," we find that as we become bondslaves, the truth does make us free indeed.

"What? know ye not that your body is the temple of the Holy Ghost which is in you, which ye have of God, and ye are not your own?" (I Cor. 6:19).

"Art thou called being a servant? care not for it: but if thou mayest be made free, use it rather" (I Cor. 7:21).

Yes, I know the song of the world says, "I wanna be free," but do those who sing it know that the way to true freedom takes them through bondage?

Let's give up the freedom to which we still cling in order to be used in helping others find that the truth shall make them free!

Poverty!

If we're different women, we own nothing and have no plans to own anything. Oh, perhaps God has given us the use of some things, but everything has been given back to Him to do with as He pleases. Our main aim is not buying and selling, fixing and gaining. My husband often asks, "Do your things possess you? Or do you possess your things? Are your things tools to help you to be used of God?"

By the time we meet the standards of the world as far as owning lands, homes, furniture, clothes, appliances, cars, campers, boats and cycles, we no longer have time to serve God. We have to wheel and deal and maintain that for which we've "wheeled and dealed."

Yes, I know! The world says, "Get ahead!" "What's he worth?" "She's worked hard and deserves all she has."

As different women, we deserve nothing; we have everything! Christ is all we need. If He's allowed you the use of money and things, give them all to God to use as He so desires. Perhaps He wants to leave them with you, but you won't care one way or the other after you've settled the issue for life.

Mrs. Russell Anderson has told me, "I believe Russell is a clearing house for some of the Lord's money. He knows He can trust Russell to be the dispatcher."

You've always thought, *I want to be rich. I want to be secure.* I can tell you how to have spiritual wealth which is the only real security in this world or the next.

First, be willing to forsake all! As the world seeks to be rich and secure, we gain spiritual riches and security in the Rock of Ages!

"And when they had brought their ships to land, they forsook all, and followed him" (Luke 5:11).

"For ye know the grace of our Lord Jesus Christ, that, though he was rich, yet for your sakes he became poor, that ye through his poverty might be rich" (II Cor. 8:9).

Suffering!

I believe it was Brother Hyles I heard say that, though we don't seek suffering, neither should we shun it.

When we give ourselves to God for service to others, we are definitely giving ourselves to a ministry of suffering. As much as we are admonished to be objective, most of us still hurt and suffer just from the very knowledge of the problems of others. Read these verses:

Matthew 16:21—"From that time forth began Jesus to shew unto his disciples, how that he must go unto Jerusalem, and suffer many things of the elders and chief priests and scribes, and be killed, and be raised again the third day."

First Corinthians 12:26—"And whether one member suffer, all the members suffer with it; or one member be honoured, all the members rejoice with it."

Second Timothy 2:21—"If a man therefore purge himself from these, he shall be a vessel unto honour, sanctified, and meet for the master's use, and prepared unto every good work."

Hebrews 13:3—"Remember them that are in bonds, as bound with them; and them which suffer adversity, as being yourselves also in the body."

First Peter 2:20, 21—"For what glory is it, if, when ye be buffeted for your faults, ye shall take it patiently? but if, when ye do well, and suffer for it, ye take it patiently, this is acceptable with God. For even hereunto were ye called: because Christ also suffered for us, leaving us an example, that ye should follow his steps."

Many take up the human cry, "If it feels good, do it," while we find if we suffer with Him, we also may be glorified together.

"The Spirit itself beareth witness with our spirit, that we are the children of God: And if children, then heirs; heirs of God, and joint-heirs with Christ; if so be that we suffer with him, that we may be also glorified together. For I reckon that the sufferings of this present time are not worthy to be compared with the glory which shall be revealed in us" (Rom. 8:16-18).

"That I may know him, and the power of his resurrection, and the fellowship of his sufferings, being made conformable unto his death" (Phil. 3:10).

The world says, "I want to feel good," which is in direct contrast to the above Scriptures.

Discipline!

I didn't quite understand Dr. Bob Jones, Sr., when he used to tell us students: "You say you don't want to take math—TAKE IT ANYWAY!" And, "You don't like greens—EAT THEM ANYWAY!" It's taken me a long time to even begin to grasp that there are only two questions to ask about anything: (1) "Is it good for me?" (2) "Is it good for others?" (which is really asking, "Is it God's plan for my life?"); and if the answer is yes, to take up His cross daily and follow Him.

"And he said to them all, If any man will come after me, let him deny himself, and take up his cross daily, and follow me" (Luke 9:23).

"I want my own way. . . to do that which is right in my own eyes. . . to do my own thing!" is diametrically opposed to all that is biblical and Christian.

Different women give up their way and in turn find that His way brings so much above and beyond their way. It brings us more than we would ever know to want.

Submission!

Different women are determined to fight the philosophy of the whole wide world in order to learn submission.

Everybody tells us we should go after "Woman Power," but we find when we forsake that cry, we receive real power—the power of God which enables us to be all He wants us to be.

Some Scriptures on submission which have helped me know God's will for me as a woman are listed here:

SUBMISSION TO GOD:

"Now be ye not stiffnecked, as your fathers were, but yield yourselves unto the Lord, and enter into his sanctuary, which he hath sanctified for ever: and serve the Lord your God, that the fierceness of his wrath may turn away from you" (II Chron. 30:8).

"Humble yourselves therefore under the mighty hand of God, that he may exalt you in due time" (I Pet. 5:6).

SUBMISSION TO HUSBAND:

"Unto the woman he said, I will greatly multiply thy sorrow and thy conception; in sorrow thou shalt bring forth children; and thy desire shall be to thy husband, and he shall rule over thee" (Gen. 3:16).

"Submitting yourselves one to another in the fear of God. Wives, submit yourselves unto your own husbands, as unto the Lord. For the husband is the head of the wife, even as Christ is the head of the church: and he is the saviour of the body" (Eph. 5:22-24).

"Nevertheless let every one of you in particular so love his wife even as himself; and the wife see that she reverence her husband" (Eph. 5:33).

"Wives, submit yourselves unto your own husbands, as it is fit in the Lord" (Col. 3:18).

"To be discreet, chaste, keepers at home, good, obedient to their own husbands, that the word of God be not blasphemed" (Titus 2:5).

"Likewise, ye wives, be in subjection to your own husbands; that, if any obey not the word, they also may without the word be won by the conversation of the wives; For after this manner in the old time the holy women also, who trusted in God, adorned themselves, being in subjection unto their own husbands" (I Pet. 3:1, 5).

SUBMISSION TO OTHER AUTHORITIES:

"Let every soul be subject unto the higher powers. For there is no power but of God: the powers that be are ordained of God. Whosoever therefore resisteth the power, resisteth the ordinance of God: and they that resist shall receive to themselves damnation. For rulers are not a terror to good works, but to the evil. Wilt thou then not be afraid of the power? do that which is good, and thou shalt have praise of the same: For he is the minister of God to thee for good. But if thou do that which is evil, be afraid; for he beareth not the sword in vain: for he is the minister of God, a revenger to execute wrath upon him that doeth evil. Wherefore ye must needs be subject, not only for wrath, but also for conscience sake. For for this cause pay ye tribute also: for they are God's ministers, attending continually upon this very thing. Render therefore to all their dues: tribute to whom tribute is due; custom to whom custom; fear to whom fear; honour to whom honour" (Rom. 13:1-7).

"Servants, obey in all things your masters according to the flesh; not with eyeservice, as menpleasers; but in singleness of heart, fearing God" (Col. 3:22).

"Let the woman learn in silence with all subjection. But I suffer not a woman to teach, nor to usurp authority over the man, but to be in silence" (I Tim. 2:11, 12).

"Put them in mind to be subject to principalities and powers, to obey magistrates, to be ready to every good work" (Titus 3:1).

"Furthermore we have had fathers of our flesh which corrected us, and we gave them reverence: shall we not much rather be in subjection unto the Father of spirits, and live?" (Heb. 12:9).

"Remember them which have the rule over you, who have spoken unto you the word of God: whose faith follow, considering the end of their conversation" (Heb. 13:7).

"Obey them that have the rule over you, and submit yourselves: for they watch for your souls, as they that must give account, that they may do it with joy, and not with grief: for that is unprofitable for you" (vs. 17).

"Salute all them that have the rule over you, and all the saints. They of Italy salute you" (vs. 24).

Femininity!

Those who wish to be different women sometimes struggle and agonize in order to become feminine as they fight the influence of the world which says, "I want my equal rights." This cry is really a tragic joke since we receive far more than equal rights as a feminine and lovely child of God.

The Women's Liberation Movement says, "You don't have to take that!" and, "They can't get by with that!"

Different women have learned that they can take anything as He takes it for them, and that "they" will not get by with anything because God has His hand on them. He'll fight our battles for us!

Purity!

The philosophy of the world tries to make us feel stupid for not taking pleasures when and where we might find them. However, I really can't say I feel stupid as I counsel hour after hour trying to help people put their lives back together after they've been wrecked by "pleasures" taken when and where they could be found.

"You live only once!" and, "I want pleasure!" seem rather trite and colorless as we see the true happiness which purity brings.

Watching a supposedly intelligent girl or woman blubbering, "Mrs. Evans, how could I have been so stupid?" has convinced me that it is intelligent to believe, "Behold, ye have sinned against the Lord: and be sure your sin will find you out" (Num. 32:23).

"If it feels good, do it!" surely does require high wages and often for a whole lifetime!

Usefulness!

"Don't volunteer for anything!" "How'd you get stuck with that job?" "Don't do anything you can get out of doing."

Recognize these statements? If they're yours, you are not different from the ordinary Christian woman! This pitiful, apathetic attitude belongs to the world, not to God's children.

"Work" and "service" are seemingly dirty words in today's society. I remember a girl telling me, "I can't erase the chalkboard for you. My folks said you get paid for that." I've often wondered how happy the girl is now that she's grown. I'm scared for those who grow up not knowing that happiness and service "go steady."

Yes, the world cries, "Take your fun in the sun," but the facts prove that she who loseth her life shall find it!!!

12 – Black Dog! White Dog! Which Shall It Be?

"Mrs. Evans, I just want to go home, put on a pair of jeans, and 'get high.' " These are words from a girl who only weeks before had said, "I am closer to the Lord than I've ever been. I never want to go back to the old ways again."

"But, Mrs. Evans, what am I going to do? My preacher left, and he isn't even preaching anymore. He led me to the Lord, he taught me every spiritual truth I've learned; what'll I do?"

I say, "He led you to whom? Then, go right on looking to that One to whom he led you."

Others tell me they really want the Christian life but honestly don't know which they'll choose since the world is calling, too.

All of these things cause me to think of the black dog and the white dog and the terrifying struggle about which we seem to know so little.

The Old Nature or the New Nature?

Do you know what I mean by a black dog and a white dog? Do you have them, too? Do you know that the first time we are going to be rid of that battle is the time we see the first glimpse of the Lord Jesus Himself? It is the battle of the old nature and the new nature, or the old man and the new man.

"If so be that ye have heard him, and have been taught by him, as the truth is in Jesus: That ye put off concerning the former conversation the old man, which is corrupt according to the deceitful lusts; And be renewed in the spirit of your mind; And that ye put on the new man, which after God is created in righteousness and true holiness" (Eph. 4:21-24).

Yes, we want a good life. We want to make Christ the Master of our lives, and yet, we pull away. You have to feed that white dog. Just imagine there is a white dog and a black dog inside you. You just have to feed that white dog with Scripture, prayer, good thoughts, soul winning, church attendance and doing good all day long by being a woman full of good works and a teacher of good things.

The white dog will be able to keep the black dog overpowered as long as you are feeding the white dog more. But you better know that the minute you stop feeding the white dog, the black dog will pounce on that white dog as the old nature takes over. As the old man takes over, he makes you look like an unsaved person.

Is it any wonder that we say, "How in the world can I think some of the things I think? Why do I do some of the things I do?"

There Are Three Kinds of People!

Do you know that Christians can surely look like the unsaved? As you understand this, your faith will not be shaken as you say, "How could they ever do such and such? They are supposed to be good Christians." Don't you understand that there are carnal Christians, spiritual Christians and unsaved people?

Dr. Jack Hyles said recently that we'd better watch the looks on our faces which can mark us as carnal Christians. You know how the kids roll their eyes to the heavens as if saying, "Oh, Mom! Are you crazy or what?" Maybe they don't dare say it, but by that roll of their eyes to the heavens appealing to God for help "with this dumb woman," you know of their disgust.

We give off our own looks of disgust. Maybe you don't appreciate everything about your husband. Maybe you wish he were just a little different. Some of you have husbands who are steady pluggers, but they are dull as all get-out. You wish sometimes that you had a man with some flair, or whatever you call it.

And then some of you have the type which one man described in this quote about himself: "I am all store front and no groceries." I mean, he comes on strong when he's up front and he's lots of fun, but you know the mess he left back home. You wish to goodness that you had someone who would just pay the bills, be steady and go straight down the line. That first look of haughty disgust should be nipped in the bud before your name becomes "carnal Christian."

Tell the Men a Thing or Two!

You know it worries me a little bit when we women have a haughty attitude. Sometimes somebody comes up to me and says, "Marlene, I wish somebody would talk to the men and tell them a thing or two!" That always makes me think, *Well, what about you? You mean to tell me that you are so straight now that we can go on to the men already?*

Sure, I know they do a lot to bring on some of the temper tantrums we have. I know they do a lot to give us the headaches we suffer. I'm sure we could list their sins from one to one hundred and never touch them all; but what a beautiful thing it would be if you just decided that you are going to be a woman used of God.

Let's say you have a drunken husband. Let's say he is horrible. What do you have to lose if you get right and are the lady of God that He tells you to be and he never gets right? You say, "It's hard!" I know it is. That's why there are only a few different women. If there were thousands, they'd no longer be different. I guarantee you the joy of being a different woman will far outweigh the price you pay to be different.

"Well, I'll shape up if he does. You talk to him! If he is ready, we'll work it out." This is not what God says. Read this:

"Likewise, ye wives, be in subjection to your own husbands; that, if any obey not the word, they also may without the word be won by the conversation of the wives; While they behold your chaste conversation coupled with fear. Whose adorning let it not be that outward adorning of plaiting the hair, and of wearing of gold, or of putting on of apparel" (I Pet. 3:1-3).

Remember the black dog and the white dog. Which will it be? Which dog are you going to feed in your life? Feeding the white dog will help you understand your husband. It will help you understand all other Christians. And it will keep you from being disappointed day after day after day.

Do you know, David is a great help to me. I just keep thinking about David. He committed sin with a woman and afterwards put her husband in battle and had him killed. That's bad! But he turned around and was used of God again. Oh, how he paid! We lose rewards, we lose joy, and we lose influence. Oh, what we lose! Oh, what David lost! But he was still used of God as the white dog took over again.

You Can't Trust People!

When you begin to understand about the black dog and the white dog, you don't say, "Well, look at her. I expected it anyway. You can't trust people, you know." No, you go right on being warm and trusting with a little "t," reserving the ultimate Trust with the big "T" for God alone but still expecting much from Christians.

You don't have to be disappointed. All you need to say when you see a Christian fall is, "Lord, help me to get into the Word. Help me to stay steady here. Help me to believe I'm in a battle, the warfare of the Spirit-filled believer. Let me see that I must have on my whole armor and be all prepared. Help me to buckle up again—just a little bit harder and a little bit tighter so that the same thing doesn't happen to me. I must remember my black dog."

Then say, "Lord, help that Christian." Don't feel bad toward that Christian, no matter what she did. You just get in there and love her and pray for her. Grab her away from the Evil One and help her to get on the track again. Help her get back to the place where she can be used of God, no matter how terrible the sin might be, no matter how much she has hurt her family or maybe a whole Christian community. That's still your time to grab hold and love her as you remember to feed your white dog.

The Dogs Are in a Battle!

"I speak after the manner of men because of the infirmity of your flesh: for as ye have yielded your members servants to uncleanness and to iniquity unto iniquity; even so now yield your members servants to righteousness unto holiness" (Rom. 6:19). You will have to decide you are in a battle. You will have to go after this thing!

"If ye then be risen with Christ, seek those things which are above, where Christ sitteth on the right hand of God. Set your affection on things above, not on things on the earth" (Col. 3:1,2). You are going to have to have a heavenly eye looking toward a heavenly calling.

"For he that soweth to his flesh shall of the flesh reap corruption; but he that soweth to the Spirit shall of the Spirit reap life everlasting" (Gal. 6:8).

"For they that are after the flesh do mind the things of the flesh; but they that are after the Spirit the things of the Spirit" (Rom. 8:5).

We could go on and on. There are so many references that I would like for you to check. Be sure to read Ephesians 6:10-18.

"Have not I commanded thee? Be strong and of a good courage; be not afraid, neither be thou dismayed: for the Lord thy God is with thee whithersoever thou goest" (Josh. 1:9).

You are in a battle, ladies! You are in a battle, girls! Let's fight the battle with the sword of the Spirit and with the Word of God fastened tight as we look unto the Author and Finisher of our faith.

Remember, ladies, there is only one thing that makes you a Christian, and that is accepting Christ for the forgiveness of your sin. He is your payment for sin that you might go to Heaven when you die. You don't work for salvation; therefore not having good works or having bad works is not going to cause you to lose your salvation. However, we'll never know on this earth how much we lose because of not working for the Lord and not giving our lives to the Lord.

But remember not to be guilty of saying, "How can they do that and be a Christian? I'm shocked and surprised. I didn't think they would ever do that." It's sad, it's heartbreaking; but it is ridiculous to keep ourselves from the knowledge that anyone is capable of anything when she feeds the black dog. As we realize that terrible potential for sin in our lives, we'll fight this thing with all we have through the power of God as we take on the whole armor of God.

I read Dr. Viola Walden's column in THE SWORD OF THE LORD one time, and I clipped this little thing from her "Scrapbook Clippings." A frightening fact:

> It might seem natural to suppose that every time a man sins he would know a little more about its nature and its method. Actually the exact reverse is true. Every time he sins he is making himself less capable of realizing that sin and is less likely to recognize that he is a sinner. For the ugly thing—and this I feel sure has never been sufficiently grasped—the really diabolical thing about sin is that it perverts a man's/woman's judgment. It stops him/her from seeing straight.

This frightening fact explains why we can be capable of anything and shows us why we as women should want to jump on little things in our own lives.

When we recognize a look of disgust on our faces, when we detect a critical spirit, when we know that we have gossiped, let's look on that as a hateful, horrible thing. Let's jump on it and stomp it and have a fit in our own lives about it so that we will never do anything worse. If we don't get on it, we soon won't be capable of seeing our sin as sin! The black dog will even look pretty.

The Dosage!

If you do not recognize the battle about which we've been writing, if you are not cognizant of the need for the Great Physician to minister a dose of Scripture, perhaps you've never accepted Christ into your life as your own personal Saviour.

We are all born into sin and can immediately cheat, steal and deceive ourselves and others with no special tutoring.

"As it is written, There is none righteous, no, not one: There is none that understandeth, there is none that seeketh after God. They are all gone out of the way, they are together become unprofitable; there is none that doeth good, no, not one" (Rom. 3:10-12).

Because of this black picture, each of us must allow the blood of Jesus to cleanse us before we even have a white dog to feed. Once we know there is a white dog, we should not yield our members as instruments of unrighteousness unto sin. "Neither yield ye your members as instruments of unrighteousness unto sin: but yield yourselves unto God, as those that are alive from the dead, and your members as instruments of righteousness unto God" (Rom. 6:13).

"And he believed in the Lord; and he counted it to him for righteousness" (Gen. 15:6).

"For if ye live after the flesh, ye shall die: but if ye through the Spirit do mortify the deeds of the body, ye shall live" (Rom. 8:13).

"The night is far spent, the day is at hand: let us therefore cast off the works of darkness, and let us put on the armour of light" (Rom. 13:12).

"By the word of truth, by the power of God, by the armour of righteousness on the right hand and on the left" (II Cor. 6:7).

"For the weapons of our warfare are not carnal, but mighty through God to the pulling down of strong holds" (II Cor. 10:4).

"For we are the circumcision, which worship God in the spirit, and rejoice in Christ Jesus, and have no confidence in the flesh. Though I might also have confidence in the flesh. If any other man thinketh that he hath whereof he might trust in the flesh, I more" (Phil. 3:3, 4).

"Continue in prayer, and watch in the same with thanksgiving" (Col. 4:2).

"Pray without ceasing. In every thing give thanks: for this is the will of God in Christ Jesus concerning you" (I Thess. 5:17,18).

"Now the Spirit speaketh expressly, that in the latter times some shall depart from the faith, giving heed to seducing spirits, and doctrines of devils" (I Tim. 4:1).

"Wherefore gird up the loins of your mind, be sober, and hope to the end for the grace that is to be brought unto you at the revelation of Jesus Christ" (I Pet. 1:13).

"For whatsoever is born of God overcometh the world: and this is the victory that overcometh the world, even our faith" (I John 5:4).

This dose of Scripture is part of the armor of God that will help you fight the battle. Please get into the fight. As we fight the black dog, we're fighting for our very lives and the lives of our children, families, churches and, yes, for America.

"Oh, to be like Jesus! All I want is to be like Him."

13 – Selective Amnesia

The greatest wonder of the world is the forgetfulness displayed by women who should remember!

As usual, we find it easy to do wrong and hard to do right! Have any of you heard that old song that used to be popular, "Doing What Comes Naturally"? I think we ought to have a song that says, "Not Doing What Comes Naturally," since those things which come naturally are usually wrong because of the depravity of man.

We just don't seem to do anything right naturally or accidentally. Everything we do right has to be planned on purpose. We have to work at doing right. We have to learn to do right. It doesn't just happen.

What is the greatest wonder of the world? Forgetfulness of women who should remember! What is the second greatest wonder of the world? The way we remember those things we should forget! Oh! Woe is me! We even have to learn what to remember and what to forget!

Remember to Forget!

Do you remember those things that you ought to have forgotten? We Christian women remember our past sins—remember them so well that we torture ourselves with them. We allow them to paralyze us instead of letting them help us be better

Christians. We use our sins to beat ourselves and make our own heads bloody. We find we can do little for others because we remember over and over those things we have done wrong.

We must remember to forget our sins! Who has forgotten our past sins if we are under the blood of the Lord Jesus Christ? God has forgotten them! Someone has said, "If you go to God to remind Him of some past confessed sin, He says, 'What do you mean? I don't know anything about it!' " God is sovereign. He is all-knowing! He is omnipresent, seeing everything, yet He has forgotten our sins because we are cleansed by the blood.

We are making Jesus' blood of no effect if we act as if Jesus' death on the cross is to no avail. When we step out to do something for the Lord and say, "Oh, no, not me! I've done (or I've been) such and such!" and then quit, we are giving the devil real victory.

You protest, "But I've committed some of these sins since I've become a Christian." Doesn't He give sincere Christians a way to take care of that? Yes, in I John 1:9: "If we confess our sins, he is faithful and just to forgive us our sins, and to cleanse us from all unrighteousness."

Forget to Remember!

Forget the past! Take that step forward. Do something for someone. Do something for God! When the devil says, "Don't you remember? Don't you remember? Get back; you are a nobody!" you step right out and say to God, "Lord, I was a nobody, but it was You who made me a somebody! You cleansed me from my sins. Even today You forgave me for a thought I didn't even know I was going to think until it was too late. You have even cleansed me from sins unknown." Psalm 19:12 says, "Who can understand his errors? cleanse thou me from secret faults."

Go ahead! Step out as far as God leads. It is not you stepping out; it is Jesus. You are just the housing for the Holy Spirit. You are nothing, but you are something because Jesus is within you. He can bless you no matter what you've done or what you've been! So forget your past sins!

"I Do Remember My Faults This Day!"

I am going to talk out of both sides of my mouth! One side of the coin is to remember to forget your sins! The other side is the only way in which we should remember our sins. Let me repeat, don't remember your sins and say, "I am a nobody. I am paralyzed. I can't do anything!"

However, positive Christian thinking might on purpose include a praise! "Lord, I know You don't even remember, but thank You for delivering me. I am going on for You!"

When you witness to someone, quickly remember where you came from and what you would be without Christ. This will help you have the right attitude about the sins of the one to whom you are talking.

It is good to bring back in remembrance your own sin in order to help you understand people with whom you are counseling. "I do remember my faults this day" (Gen. 41:9). Ask yourself, "Lord, what have I done that is similar to this?" He will then allow it to come back in memory so you can know how to help others.

Do You Remember the Bad?

Sometimes people remember only the bad things you do to them. How many of you who have been married for a long time have more bad memories than good ones? Now, if you do remember the good, how have you helped yourself remember the good and gotten victory over the bad? If your husband has been taken away through death or been away because of work, perhaps it has been easier to dwell on the good things. It's a shameful fact that we don't fully appreciate those whom we have.

Do you remember when you moved from your parents' home? What did you remember the most? Was it Mom saying, "Get this room picked up"? Or did you look back and remember the good things after you had been away for awhile? Usually, we have to get away from home to remember the good things. Men who have gone into service write about how glad they are for their wonderful home. Did they appreciate it when they were there?

We need to decide on purpose to remember the good and forget the bad in order not to lose what we have.

What good does it do to remember the bad anyway? Remembering the bad is only good if it will spur you on to do better. If something bad has happened in your marriage, will dwelling on it help? No! In fact, it will hurt a whole lot. Depraved people think about the bad. But it is natural for one to dwell on that.

Perhaps sharing a letter I wrote to a lady wanting to know how she could regain her husband's love will point out what we're saying here.

> You say you are separated from your husband but that you want to get him back and you feel this is what he wants since he continues to talk to you.
>
> The fact that you're going through the stage when he wants nothing to do with the marriage or with a divorce means you have a period in which to go to work to restore your fellowship with him. From my opportunities to counsel, I have learned that this stage of doubt will last only a few months. If you want him, go after him by not going after him.
>
> Most women use this period of time in a way which really kills off any possibilities of the marriage being restored. They insist on a long time of "talking it out" as they question, wheedle, accuse and humiliate. They "give him what he deserves" and they get a divorce. It's not a very good deal to live with for life.
>
> I believe the only thing you can do is to begin again to rejoice in the Lord. If your main rejoicing has not been in your husband but in the Lord, you are still able to rejoice. The main thing that would bring him back would be your rejoicing heart.
>
> I truly believe the only way you will win him is to be a lot of fun, enjoy him, give him no correction, no innuendoes or insinuations, or even a condemning look. He probably does not deserve this kind of treatment, but we do not deserve the treatment God gives us when we err and He loves us back into His way.

If he does not want you to touch him or to try in any way to show affection, just let him make the moves. As he comes to see you, just be as if you were a girl on a casual date with someone you liked. Now, maybe it is not worth it. That has to be up to you.

Please get into the Word of God and let the Lord Jesus Christ be your lover. In that way you will not be as bitter, resentful or ugly as you might otherwise be. You need Him more now, not less, yet you say you are slipping away from the Lord because of what has taken place.

This is your time to show what kind of Christian you are. Outward difficult circumstances cause a good Christian to just cuddle up closer to the Lord Jesus. You say, "This is hard!" You'd better believe it! The Holy Spirit can help you do it if you will allow Him.

You call the women "friends" who tell you he is with another woman. I do not call them friends; I call them gossips. If any of your so-called friends start with that again, hurriedly raise your hand and tell them you have no need to know these things.

If he is with another woman, there is nothing you can do about it. The worst thing you can do is to confront him and cause him to deny it. If he hasn't been with another woman, he may go get one, probably figuring that if he has the name, he might as well have the game. He doesn't need your suggestion for sin.

Please do not listen to your "friends," nor even discuss the situation with them. Most "friends" tell you what they think you want to hear, then run to someone else to tell them a different story. Go to one counselor, perhaps your pastor or an older woman, who will confidentially comfort you and help you to straighten up, get right and grow into the woman the Lord wants you to be, even if you never get your husband back.

I know you are saying, "Mrs. Evans, you don't understand. You haven't gone through this." You're right, I don't and I haven't—but I know God's Word is true and that I'm giving Bible-taught thoughts I've seen work whenever anyone has used them. I am just pointing you to the Word and to the God of the Word who makes these things work. I can only pray that in whatever He allows to happen to me, I will follow His Word. If I don't, it still makes it no less true.

You can sit around and feel sorry for yourself and have a big pity-party, or you can use this to go the Lord's way in praying and having the peace of God that He will work this thing out in His time, His purpose, His will and for His glory.

My message to you consists of two words I've been saying

> to myself for a long, long time, and they are very effective. I would not say them to your face, but I suggest that you say them to your own self: "Shut Up!" We are all too verbal sometimes.
>
> You may think this is hard and cold, but if it helps you, I will have been the warmest heart of all—yes, a real friend.

Married people remember, listen to and dwell on only the bad, even when they say they're willing to pay any price to help the marriage. Roommates who are having trouble are going to remember everything bad that has happened through the year. For example I heard this:

"Back in October (October 2), my mother sent me a box containing a whole lot of goodies. I let everybody eat from it. My roommate had all she wanted. On November 3rd she got a box, and you know what she did? She hid it!" The girl is telling me this in March! She remembered the bad the roommate did and the good she herself did.

Forget the Good You Do!

Women, forget the good you do! Try to forget your good works! Let's remember to forget! Let's have selective amnesia! Select what you are going to forget. Forgetting your good works now will assure you of having them in Heaven.

"Let your light so shine before men, that they may see your good works, and glorify your Father which is in heaven" (Matt. 5:16).

"But lay up for yourselves treasures in heaven, where neither moth nor rust doth corrupt, and where thieves do not break through nor steal" (Matt. 6:20).

If you parade what you do for others, they are not going to want you to do anything for them, saying, "We will hear about it for the rest of our lives," or, "I'll be obligated to her." If you do it for Jesus, you will never drag your good works out to show people! So forget your good works; you've given them to Jesus.

If I give something to you, I am not literally giving it to you but to the Lord! Outside of the Holy Spirit and the Word of God, people are all I know of the fruit of the Spirit—joy, peace, gentleness, longsuffering. All that comes out of people is my picture of Jesus. "Inasmuch as ye have done it unto one of the least of these my brethren, ye have done it unto me" (Matt. 25:40).

Forget what you do for others, but remember every little thing others do for you!

Now, ladies, I am asking for a miracle to happen in our lives when I ask you never to say, "Look what I did for her; and now look what she is doing!" But remember—you didn't do it for her; you did it for Jesus!

Be wise with your time and money! If you are giving it to God as wisely as you know how, what happens to those you are helping is God's business! You need never feel cheated. If the people you are helping do wrong, or if they treat you badly, you'll feel, "I've been taken! I've been had!" No, you haven't. You will meet your gifts again if you gave them to Jesus. Besides, no one knows what will happen to the one you helped. The records aren't all in yet. The accounts are not settled. Miracles happen every day, so let's count on their happening!

Forget What People Do Wrong!

Doing what comes naturally is to retaliate and spread gossip. When you don't do what comes naturally, you have selective amnesia in order to forget those things you should not remember. You will be blessed for this!

One day some woman in the church calls your pastor-husband and lambastes him up one side and down the other. The natural thing would be for you to despise her. But don't do what comes naturally. At church you greet her: "Hi, Mrs. Jones. How are you today?" Do what comes unnaturally. Be abnormal! Be unnatural! The Holy Spirit is living in you, and so you must treat her the way Christ would treat her. Jesus said, "He that is without sin among you, let him first cast a stone at her" (John 8:7).

If you have some adverse feelings toward somebody, write down ten good things you have seen her do and write down ten times when you have had good interchange or fun-times with her. Then check your feelings again. Set your mind on the good and go toward the good until you gain something akin to like for that person. Perhaps you will even catch yourself loving her!

Sometimes I hear myself say, *I don't see how they could do such and such,* forgetting all about the time I did something just like it or failing to remember a sin of mine parallel to theirs. I don't know how any of us is qualified to say, "I don't understand how she could do such and such," since we all are capable of doing the most wicked things under the proper conditions. Why wouldn't you think she could do such and such? She is a depraved person, but saved by the blood of the Lord Jesus Christ just like the rest of us.

There are times when you must recall the sins of others in order to help them, but this is in an attitude of love and prayer and completely different from what we're discussing.

Some people sin differently than others. There are those who can take quiet sinners better than loud sinners. They prefer the sinner to hide the sin and be sly about it. But there is really no difference. Sin is sin! Others may say, "I respect her. At least she comes out with it and tells it like it is."

The best way is to accept every sinner, remembering that every Christian is a sinner saved by grace. Succumb to the lovely disease of selective amnesia, "forgetting" the sin in order to be to them what Jesus is to you.

I believe Jesus has selective amnesia. I believe God has selected to forget our sins. So let us be like Him and do that for others.

"As far as the east is from the west, so far hath he removed our transgressions from us" (Ps. 103:12).

14 – Give Yourself Away!

As we hear songs and stories about the greatest Gift of all, let us learn to give ourselves away! Don't you often wonder aloud, *What could I ever do for Jesus to show Him how much I love Him for giving Himself for me?* I have—and I think I know the answer, although I am afraid I do not practice it consistently: "GIVE YOURSELF AWAY!" You ask, "How?" God gives us examples through His birth, life, death, burial and resurrection.

Give Yourself to the Word of God!

Most of us are so ignorant of the Word of God that we think the term "give yourself away" is strange. Supposedly even mature Christians sometimes think living a life without retaliation or with strong separation is weird. Because our thinking is determined by what we allow to enter our minds, the worldly seems right and the spiritual seems wrong. "There is a way which seemeth right unto a man, but the end thereof are the ways of death" (Prov. 14:12).

When I'd want to go to a school dance or something similar, my mom would tell me, "Grandma Wilkins always said the church is dancing into the world and the world is dancing into the church until you can't see the difference." As I sulked away thinking, *Grandma Wilkins Schmilkins. . . who cares what some old lady said? She's dead anyway! She didn't know anything,* little did I know I'd someday be begging Christian young people to set their affection on things above and be hid with Christ in God.

"If ye then be risen with Christ, seek those things which are above, where Christ sitteth on the right hand of God. Set your affection on things above, not on things on the earth. For ye are dead, and your life is hid with Christ in God" (Col. 3:1-4).

Scores of times each day I say, *That doesn't sound right.* I realize I don't know what is right and what is wrong because I'm so ignorant of the only Book that can teach me eternal rights and wrongs. Oh, yes, I've studied the Book, read through it, and I love it. However, considering the number of years I've been saved, I'm relatively unlearned. Are you? Hey, then, I know something we can give Jesus. We can give ourselves to His Word.

The fact that I did not give myself to the Word earlier in life has been my saddest regret. Once when I was evaluating the number of Scripture verses I would know if my Bible were ever taken from me, I found that I was pitifully lacking.

I have been trying to live in the Word, but my way of "living in the Word" seems so simple that I've been embarrassed to tell it. However, I'm beginning to think my little way is better than your way, if you have no way at all. Maybe my way would be a start for those of you who are still complaining, "I don't have time to live in the Word," or, "I just don't understand the Bible," or, "I read the Bible for awhile, but then I don't get anything from it and quit."

I know; I've been through that off-again, on-again syndrome that goes something like this: No Bible. . . a revival meeting . . . read Bible avidly for three days. . . read Bible one day but unable to concentrate or get anything from it. . . give up. . . no Bible. . . revival. . . then again I read Bible for three days. . . ad nauseam.

Today people don't have character enough to do something if they aren't receiving something from what they are doing. They quit! The worldly philosophy even tells us to be true to ourselves by giving up that which doesn't mean anything to us.

I want to tell you—I've kept some good habits that have helped me even when I wasn't sincere. True, we should find a way to read the Bible until it does mean something, but we're commanded to stay in it whether we get anything from it or not. "Study to shew thyself approved unto God, a workman that needeth not to be ashamed, rightly dividing the word of truth" (II Tim. 2:15).

However, since we are all horribly affected by the world, it is even more important that we allow the Holy Spirit to teach us and reach us through His Word. We need to be thrilled, excited, as we get our joys, laughs, tears, shocks, facts, truths and everything else from the Scriptures. "But shun profane and vain babblings: for they will increase unto more ungodliness. And their word will eat as doth a canker" (II Tim. 3:16,17).

You still want to know my way? I don't know if I want to tell you! Well—okay, I will. I read just a few verses instead of many chapters. And I ask myself questions about those few verses: *What does this mean? How does it apply to me? Does this mean like the time I did such and such?* Then I sit and let my mind wander on purpose, just visiting with the Lord.

One day when meditating on John 14:1-7, I specialized on mansions—thinking about those I have seen on earth and thanking Him for mine I can't even imagine in Heaven. I thanked the Lord for a trip to the Arbor Lodge Mansion in Nebraska City, Nebraska, and prayed for the people who took me on that trip. . . my parents! Then I thought of someone who doesn't have a heavenly mansion because she's not saved. I prayed for her.

I know we need a prayer list so we will pray for all those for whom we promised to pray. We also need to have Bible study. However, this grabbing a few verses, or even a portion of one small verse, to chew on all day will thrill your heart, cause you to glory in the Word and provoke you to further study.

One day while dwelling in Philippians 3:10, especially on the phrase, "that I may know him," I spent every few hours thinking about and praising God for a different way through which I knew Him. I could see Him really well every way I turned.

I remember spending a week in Romans 8:35-39 which features sheep. I thought to pray for people who came to my mind for the first time in years as I recalled the one time I saw a sheep shearing on a farm in Thayer, Kansas. I also prayed for the peoples of India, Africa and Asia as I spent some time considering the word *famine.*

I let Him talk to me through His Word, and I talk to Him about that which His Word reminds me. It's just like talking to a friend. My Friend says something that reminds me to tell Him something. I even interrupt Him! You see, Jesus and I are pretty close!

Many of us run through six chapters and a prayer list in such a perfunctory manner. No way can we possibly get anything from it. This method is sort of like running up to a friend and saying, "I got your letter. I'll skip through it. 'Bye now." She would think you crazy, and that kind of relationship wouldn't last long. Neither will your relationship with God last if it is carried on through these puny methods.

Stop, think out each word, speak the phrase aloud, draw out a word such as *all* in "I can do *all* things . . ."; then ask yourself, *How can I do all things?* Answer yourself: *"Through Christ." Who does what? "Who strengtheneth me!"*

Dear me! I'm letting you know how much I talk to myself again! Well, there's no help for it!

Give Yourself to People

This, too, is an old concept—old as the Bible for sure, yet one which seems strange to the world (even the Christian world) today! Democracy as a way of government has been revered until the theme has also been adopted as a way of living. Our great statements spout out like mighty gushers: "I've got my rights!" "I'm not going to kowtow to anybody!" "I'm just as good as the other guy!" "Who was his servant last year!" Some statements have been so overused that the biblical thinking on servitude and following counsel are, even among the most devout Christians, all but extinct.

Do you ever notice how uncomfortable some folks become when people voluntarily place themselves in the position of a servant? Some of that "I-don't-want-anyone-waiting-on-me" stuff comes from strict training concerning doing for self. Perhaps while we train folks to do for themselves, we ought to also teach gracious acceptance of help when others have a need to give it.

I believe another reason for their being uncomfortable is that they identify with the "servant." Feeling they should be willing to serve but finding themselves not willing, they put the whole idea down. I'm afraid this feeling sorry for the voluntary servant means we don't really believe, "Inasmuch as ye have done it unto one of the least of these my brethren, ye have done it unto me" (Matt. 25:40).

Now, I know there are dangers in this. In fact, there is a danger in every truth or good thing, for, if taken to excess, any good can be spoken evil of. One danger is that some are not at all bothered if someone serves them. They spend their lives waiting to be waited on or served. They think the world owes them a living, as well as a servant.

Another danger is that of poor self-esteem. This makes a full-time slave out of one who feels he/she must pay his/her way to be worthy to be around others. You've seen the lady who never sits down to visit following a meal in another's home; she is the self-appointed maid before and after any and every event. Such a one may be covering her social inadequacy by giving in to this need to prove herself worthy through "making her way." This will keep her from developing strengths which she needs.

However, I do love to see a girl or lady go into the home of a friend and insist on taking over all kitchen duties and serving the meal. You say, "Oh, I couldn't do that." Or perhaps the host would say, "I'd feel funny letting someone do that at my house." Why?

We've been brainwashed by the world to believe this type thing is degrading and humiliating; therefore, it is possible neither party would feel comfortable enough to enjoy this. It's a shame that some of us don't know how to give ourselves, and some of us don't know how to graciously accept the gift of servitude (not enforced slavery) from another.

For eight years I had the privilege of being a waitress in my parents' restaurant. Then I spent many years (off and on) in restaurants (such as one belonging to a Highland Park Baptist Church family in Chattanooga), and the dining hall of a college. There's something mighty good about that training. You're there to please a group of people, and you are usually rewarded according to how you serve.

Matthew 25:21 tells us, "His lord said unto him, Well done, thou good and faithful servant: thou hast been faithful over a few things, I will make thee ruler over many things: enter thou into the joy of thy lord."

As a waitress, your reward is immediate. When I started teaching, I was paid by the month. This just about killed me, since I had been accustomed to getting money after each individual serving of a table! I loved having my pockets full of money every day! I'd get them pretty full, too, if I jumped to meet people's needs before they knew they had them, kept my mouth shut even if they griped, arranged the table attractively and smiled pleasantly.

Today they say that type thing is out of style, but since I want my pockets full of blessings, I "ain't gonna" believe it! By the time the world retracts this philosophy, I'll have my pockets full of blessings! The world always has had a difficult time knowing what to believe. Isn't it good to have a Bible!

Now, I try to give myself to my husband, children and the girls at Hyles-Anderson College. It's something like servitude—voluntary but still servitude. Truly giving myself is averting my eyes from things around me, or ideas within me, in order to give full attention to those with whom I'm dealing. Most children receive so little satisfying attention at home that, as our preacher says, "They're hungry for us."

There are words and phrases which help me learn to concentrate on the person at hand. "Blinders" makes me think of horses and the keeping of eyes "straight ahead," "to the work," "on the job." And I like to "zero in." I will influence my children and Hyles-Anderson College girls and be a real source of comfort and blessing to my husband only as I learn the meaning of these words.

We have to practice giving ourselves to others, because giving to one person helps us in giving to the next one. It's the law of using or losing. Elaine Colsten teaches us to write down distracting thoughts in order to be able to forget anything which would take our minds from the person to whom we are committed.

Most of us have spent our lives thinking about the past (which we cannot change), or the future (which we cannot control), and have rarely given ourselves to anyone in the present . . . the here and now.

"But seek ye first the kingdom of God, and his righteousness; and all these things shall be added unto you. Take therefore no thought for the morrow: for the morrow shall take thought for the things of itself. Sufficient unto the day is the evil thereof" (Matt. 6:33, 34).

Yes, we sat in geography class worrying about history; twisted in history class because we were concerned about English; and spent English class preparing for math. Now, we plan dinner during church services and use dinner time to worry about supper.

"For God so loved the world, that he gave his only begotten Son, that whosoever believeth in him should not perish, but have everlasting life" (John 3:16). God gave—and so can you!

First, have you given yourself to His plan of salvation (the only one)? "That if thou shalt confess with thy mouth the Lord Jesus, and shalt believe in thine heart that God hath raised him from the dead, thou shalt be saved. For with the heart man believeth unto righteousness; and with the mouth confession is made unto salvation" (Rom. 10:9,10).

Second, have you given yourself completely to Him? Have you presented (given) yourself as a living sacrifice?

"I beseech you therefore, brethren, by the mercies of God, that ye present your bodies a living sacrifice, holy, acceptable unto God, which is your reasonable service. And be not conformed to this world: but be ye transformed by the renewing of your mind, that ye may prove what is that good, and acceptable, and perfect, will of God" (Rom. 12:1, 2).

Third, have you given yourself to Him through His Word? Today?

"Thy words were found, and I did eat them; and thy word was unto me the joy and rejoicing of mine heart: for I am called by thy name, O Lord God of hosts" (Jer. 15:16).

Fourth, are you giving yourself to others?

"He that findeth his life shall lose it: and he that loseth his life for my sake shall find it" (Matt. 10:39).

Give yourself away!

15 – Mind Control

Because we (mankind) have been blessed with a mind far superior to all other forms of God's creation, life doesn't have to just happen to us. We can happen to life! Yes we can, even in time of difficulty.

God has given us a free will: "And the Spirit and the bride say, Come. And let him that heareth say, Come. And let him that is athirst come. And whosoever will, let him take the water of life freely" (Rev. 22:17).

He has given us all of nature: "Because that which may be known of God is manifest in them; for God hath shewed it unto them. For the invisible things of him from the creation of the world are clearly seen, being understood by the things that are made, even his eternal power and Godhead; so that they are without excuse" (Rom. 1:19, 20).

He has also given us the Word of God: "All scripture is given by inspiration of God, and is profitable for doctrine, for reproof, for correction, for instruction in righteousness" (II Tim. 3:16).

All Scripture has been given in order that we might be able to choose Him as Saviour: "Not by works of righteousness which we have done, but according to his mercy he saved us, by the washing of regeneration, and renewing of the Holy Ghost; Which he shed on us abundantly through Jesus Christ our Saviour;

That being justified by his grace, we should be made heirs according to the hope of eternal life" (Titus 3:5-7).

Scripture has been given that we might love Him as Lord: "Jesus said unto him, Thou shalt love the Lord thy God with all thy heart, and with all thy soul, and with all thy mind" (Matt. 22:37).

Once we have made Him our Saviour and crowned Him Lord, we can begin to show Him our love by "bringing into captivity every thought to the obedience of Christ" (II Cor. 10:5). No parent, preacher, friend or teacher can do this for us. They can give us good thoughts on which to dwell, but we have to do the dwelling. No person can control your mind for you. God could have chosen to control our minds, of course, but He did not do so. He gave us a mind—the most fantastic machine in all the world: "Let this mind be in you, which was also in Christ Jesus" (Phil. 2:5).

He inspired the Word of God for an "instruction book" on how to operate the machine: "And be not conformed to this world: but be ye transformed by the renewing of your mind, that ye may prove what is that good, and acceptable, and perfect, will of God" (Rom. 12:2).

He even provided preachers and teachers: "And though the Lord give you the bread of adversity, and the water of affliction, yet shall not thy teachers be removed into a corner any more, but thine eyes shall see thy teachers: And thine ears shall hear a word behind thee, saying, This is the way, walk ye in it, when ye turn to the right hand, and when ye turn to the left" (Isa. 30:20, 21). He did all this to help us understand the BOOK, but we have to take it from there.

Perhaps you are questioning the fact that you have a fantastic machine, especially if you have just taken an I.Q. test or received a report card of some sort. Stop it! The poorest, weakest mind is a marvelous creation!

Now that we have acknowledged our good machine—the

mind—and have established the fact that we can control it by God's grace, how do we go about it?

Substitute Thinking!

My favorite practice of mind control is substitute thinking, as outlined in Philippians 4:8: "Finally, brethren, whatsoever things are true, whatsoever things are honest, whatsoever things are just, whatsoever things are pure, whatsoever things are lovely, whatsoever things are of good report; if there be any virtue, and if there be any praise, think on these things."

God is so good: He isn't like us. We tell our children to be good, thresh them over for having bad attitudes, yell at them for not practicing scriptural thinking; but we completely fail to show and tell them how to attain all this.

In Philippians 4:4-8, our Father tells us to rejoice always, to let our moderation be known, and to be careful for nothing. He even tells us what we'll get for doing all that—peace of God; and, then, lo and behold, He tells us the "how" for what He told us to do!

I tell young people what and give them "what for," but I often forget to tell them "how." Well, what I get from Philippians 4:4-8 is this: If I see something impure, I should quickly grab a pure thought and superimpose it upon my mind. I think that means that if I should unavoidably see a "dirty" bumper sticker on the car in front of me, I should lift my eyes away from it while I quickly give thanks for a lovely pure lady of my acquaintance.

Here's another one: If someone gives me a bad report (gossip) before I can stop her, I believe I should quickly give some good report to the talebearer. Surely this practice can keep my mind from becoming any more cluttered and dirty than it already is. You know I already feel that ". . . the good that I would I do not: but the evil which I would not, that I do" (Rom. 7:19).

Please study the following verses from Romans 7:15-25:

"For that which I do I allow not: for what I would, that do I not; but what I hate, that do I. If then I do that which I would not, I consent unto the law that it is good. Now then it is no more I that do it, but sin that dwelleth in me. For I know that in me (that is in my flesh,) dwelleth no good thing: for to will is present with me; but how to perform that which is good I find not. For the good that I would I do not: but the evil which I would not, that I do. Now if I do that I would not it is no more I that do it, but sin that dwelleth in me. I find then a law, that, when I would do good, evil is present with me. For I delight in the law of God after the inward man: but I see another law in my members, warring against the law of my mind, and bringing me into captivity to the law of sin which is in my members. O wretched man that I am! who shall deliver me from the body of this death? I thank God through Jesus Christ our Lord. So then with the mind I myself serve the law of God; but with the flesh the law of sin."

There are a couple of other mind-control exercises which are really nothing but another way to use substitute thinking. One is what I call the "magnifying principle." We either see the water glass half full or half empty; we either take people on a downer or an upper; we represent givers or takers. In my mind, I make my right side the bright and good side and the left side, the dark and wrong side; then I train a big imaginary magnifying glass on the right side most of the time. Once in awhile I regress and have to switch hands mentally so that I can magnify the right side again.

Now I realize all this sounds very infantile, but since it helps me, I won't apologize. Being negative is acting pretty infantile, so maybe we need to use kindergarten methods to combat kindergarten behavior; suppose so?

I often thank the Lord for the blocking-out mechanism He has given me. That is the other substitute-thinking exercise to which I referred earlier. The first time I was consciously aware of using it was the time of my grandma's death when I was in the ninth grade.

She had been terribly ill with cancer for many months, but on that New Year's Eve of 1948 I still was not ready to accept her death. So I didn't. In fact, I had a big time celebrating the arrival of the New Year even after I was told about Grandma's Homegoing.

Because I really loved her, I felt some guilt. I remember puzzling over my strange actions. Of course, now I know I was rejecting the truth. Once I had time to accept it, more normal reactions began to take place.

I'm not usually given to hysteria, yelling, screaming or handwringing. I attribute that blessing to God's goodness in allowing me to use the "blocking-out mechanism" of my brain until such time as I can accept those mind-boggling things that happen around me.

Do not misunderstand: feelings must be faced, and His grace is sufficient. "And he said unto me, My grace is sufficient for thee: for my strength is made perfect in weakness. Most gladly therefore will I rather glory in my infirmities, that the power of Christ may rest upon me" (II Cor. 12:9). He surely does give "more grace when the burdens grow greater," just as the songwriter expresses.

The following verse seems to indicate that facing our wrong feelings and admitting them (to ourselves and even to others) can lead to prayer for one another, and this in turn can cause us to be healed: "Confess your faults one to another, and pray one for another, that ye may be healed. The effectual fervent prayer of a righteous man availeth much" (James 5:16).

Did you ever hide something so well that you couldn't find it? Most of us are so busy hiding our sins from others that we can't even find the hiding place in order to face and deal with the problem. This is using the blocking-out mechanism in a harmful way, which will cause us to remain spiritual dwarfs.

How many times have you admitted to yourself that you were jealous? When my mother would tell me about some girl she knew from my school who was supposedly a fine girl, I always countered, "Mom, if you just knew her! She's really bad!" Never do I remember saying to myself, *I am jealous!*

Did you ever try to figure out why you don't want to give attention to someone who seemingly begs for it? You know what I mean. You've had someone tell one big story after another, all of which you suspected were figments of the imagination.

Perhaps you've had another person start asking you questions about herself which seem to be designed to program you to give her compliments. In these cases, has your mind worked like this? *All she wants is attention, so just see if I say anything nice to her.*

Since our mental processes can always be counted on to proceed to the carnal, I wonder if we ought not re-evaluate. Ought we plan how to go against our feelings and perform the unnatural by using some spiritual character? You say, "But she never seems to get enough attention." Then she must need more, and it is our privilege to be unselfish enough to give it.

Our Minds Are Warped!

Remember, our minds play tricks on us. Unless you ". . . be renewed in the spirit of your mind" (Eph. 4:23), you can plan on poor, warped thinking. Some of you, "having the understanding darkened," are "alienated from the life of God through the ignorance . . ." (Eph. 4:18). "This I say therefore, and testify in the Lord, that ye henceforth walk not as other Gentiles walk, in the vanity of their mind" (vs. 17).

If you don't know whether or not you're going to Heaven when you die, your mind is not just warped; it's completely blinded! "But if our gospel be hid, it is hid to them that are lost: In whom the god of this world hath blinded the minds of them which believe not, lest the light of the glorious gospel of Christ, who is the image of God, should shine unto them" (II Cor. 4:3, 4).

Christians have so much difficulty trying to live both the spiritual and fleshly life that we sometimes appear schizophrenic. This can be helped by James 4:8, "Draw nigh to God, and he will draw nigh to you. Cleanse your hands, ye sinners; and purify your hearts, ye double minded." To get biblical thinking, you may have to give up your way of thinking completely. This may take a miracle, for it may necessitate admitting you are wrong.

To say your thought processes have been trained to follow the wrong groove is to say you need to be "brain-cleansed" by God, His Word and His people. The devil will fight that. "But I fear, lest by any means, as the serpent beguiled Eve through his subtilty, so your minds should be corrupted from the simplicity that is in Christ" (II Cor. 11:3).

Yes, it is right to repeat and go over in your mind Bible-taught thoughts and principles: "Do what you don't want to do; go against your feelings." This will help you in that the right groove will be there when the situation arises. Your mind will be so spiritually conditioned that you will react with New Testament love to things, problems and people.

Let me warn you that it won't seem right, because so little pure New Testament love has been practiced and displayed in our generation.

How Did It Happen?

One of the questions I've most often heard in my years of counseling girls has been, "Mrs. Evans, how did it happen?"

Look at the progression of sin taught in Psalm 1. Dr. Bob Jones, Sr., said a man doesn't rob a bank overnight, because the process of wicked thinking has to work. "For as he thinketh in his heart, so is he . . ." (Prov. 23:7). First, he might have thought as he passed a bank, *A man could rob that bank easily.* Then, *Here's how a man could rob that bank.* Finally, *I am going to rob that bank.*

Our beautiful God-given mind can work for our good and His glory, or it can rationalize, adapt and adjust to sin in such a way that we can really believe right is wrong and black is white. The difference depends upon who is in control of your mind.

If you are in trouble, how did you get there? Mother, if your daughter is impure, try to remember how it started. No young girl grows up thinking, *When I'm older I want to hurt my parents, or have my first physical experience of love in the back seat of a car.* She thinks it "just happened," but you and I know better, don't we?

Did it begin when you were too busy to regulate the phone calls you thought were so innocent? After all, what wrong can one do on the phone? Plenty, that's what! Hours of breathing sweet nothings into seeming space provides the familiarity that makes it possible to build a bridge in days—when that bridge should take months, even years, to build.

First, he said, "I'd like to hold you." Then, "I'm tired of fighting this. It isn't working." (Of course it isn't when they're putting all their minds only on one another.) Next comes, "I think we can get together alone. Nothing will happen." Do I need to describe the turning of the wheels from that point to, "If you love me, you'll let me"? It's a rare girl who can at this stage say, "If you love me, you won't let me let you."

It could have been controlled way back when. Mom and Dad could have appeared stupid, crazy and old-fashioned as they insisted on limited phone conversations, carefully regulated dates and an open-door (open to parents) policy. Where in the world did we ever get the idea that teenage daughters deserve all kinds of unbelievable privacy in order to carry on dating routines? Again, the world has duped us.

One night my husband and I were called to the home of a hysterical couple who had just discovered that their teenage daughter (who they said had never caused any problems) was in deep trouble, legally and physically, because of drugs.

The girl told us she had kept the drugs in her room for two years. Her parents told us, "We respected her privacy"!

I'm not advocating being a prison warden, but almost! You see, if we put ourselves and those for whom we're responsible "in prison," God and other people won't have to do so. I'd rather my kids be popular with the neighbors than that I be popular with my kids.

I used to tell a girl at Hyles-Anderson College, "Let me put you in prison (discipline and rules); put your own self in prison, then others will let you out. Be hard on yourself, then others won't have to be hard on you."

That girl did allow me to put her "in prison"; she also put herself "in prison" for two long years. Now every door of Christian service she could ever want is open to her. Of course, the habit of keeping herself in prison is now so firmly established that she continues to gain from imprisonment.

It just doesn't seem right, does it? It's just biblical thinking of which we're so ignorant. "Put yourself last; He'll put you first. Die so that you can really live."

Once Dr. Hyles preached to us about the visual aids his mother used to help teach him the truth—that if he'd wear a wooden yoke, he wouldn't ever have to wear a yoke of iron.

"Go and tell Hananiah, saying, Thus saith the Lord; Thou hast broken the yokes of wood; but thou shalt make for them yokes of iron. For thus saith the Lord of hosts, the God of Israel; I have put a yoke of iron upon the neck of all these nations, that they may serve Nebuchadnezzar king of Babylon; and they shall serve him: and I have given him the beasts of the field also" (Jer. 28:13, 14).

All of this really makes sense to me, but I still don't believe it enough to apply it in every area of my own life. Think of this: Put yourself in prison at the dinner table, and you'll be out of prison at the dress shop!

If you will put yourself in prison by never getting into a car alone with a man to whom you're not married, you will probably have a better chance of not being in the prison house of divorce.

Do you suppose this thinking is why God made such statements as, "Look not on a woman to commit adultery," and why He likened hate to murder?

You look, you lust, you act; you think, you want, you like, you believe you have the right! This is the way it goes because we are what we think, and we are in the process of becoming what we think. Where your mind goes, your heart, speech and body will follow!

The Decision Is Yours!

The decision is yours. He has loved you to Himself and given you His Book, but what you do about it is your decision. It is not enough to say, "I have decided to follow Jesus." How are you going to follow Him? You decide how you will react and what you will do when the first little step to sin creeps in. If you jump on it while it can be controlled, folks (I mean good Christians) are going to say you are crazy. If you plan on their thinking you are crazy, you won't be thrown out of kilter by that. Keep smelling salts on hand in case you get encouragement from some rare individual.

Let me tell you something! If you allow yourself to be swayed by public opinion (even good Christian public opinion) and you get into trouble, let me know how many of those good Christians come to help and comfort you.

Don't just say, "I tried to do right, but it didn't work out." Make a formula of success for every decision. If you don't know how, watch someone who is successful in the area of your new commitment. What do they do? Does it line up with the Bible? Decision: "I'm going to be pure for life." How? 1. Bible thinking; 2. Rules; 3. Long hard hours of work; 4. New interest; and 5. Good activity.

Go ahead! Put the "what" under points of the "how."

What rules will you impose upon yourself? They need to be harder than any church or school can make or enforce. Some dastardly deeds have been committed on chaperoned youth group parties sponsored by fundamental, Bible-believing, soul-winning churches. Terrible habits have been begun at Christian camps and schools.

Life doesn't just happen to you. Your thinking programs your life, and the five senses program your thinking. Therefore, your thinking is determined by what you see, hear, smell, taste and touch!

"Be sober, be vigilant; because your adversary the devil, as a roaring lion, walketh about, seeking whom he may devour" (I Pet. 5:8).

Put yourself "in prison" so God can let you out!!

16 – The Atmosphere Is Up to You!

One day we who work with *Christian Womanhood* asked for an appointment with Elaine Colsten and named her "consultant"! She jokingly said, "I'll be an 'ornery' member of your team."

I just have to tell you, she is sharp! Besides that, we like her a whole lot. She's unusual in that she's so smart, yet she doesn't make us feel dumb.

We were discussing the college girls when I asked her, "Elaine, can't the girls kind of set the tone of the school in making it easier for the guys to be the leaders?" She quickly replied, "Oh, yes, of course, just as a woman sets the atmosphere of the home."

That started me thinking: *There are men who are such natural-born leaders that they are going to lead, no matter what. However, most young men need a conducive atmosphere in which to become the leaders they were meant to be.*

And with that I began a study on atmosphere.

Kris Grafton, a staff member of Hyles-Anderson College, hurriedly looked up the word in the dictionary. And what she found provided me with food for thought. I hope you will use it as food for the heart.

Atmosphere Is Air Surrounding the Earth!

Girls and women can become the atmosphere which is life-giving support to a leader, bus captain, preacher, teacher, dad or husband. Just as the earth could not continue in existence without the atmosphere, just so we are that important to every situation and person with whom we interact.

Watch a good woman walk into a restaurant, perhaps one in which even a rowdy party is taking place. Check the change in atmosphere as she moves in the beauty of the Lord. I don't say it will happen every time, but it will happen.

Next time you go to a shopping mall, sit and study people for awhile. Watch a gum-chewing, jeans-wearing, hip-swinging girl meet a group of friends; note the effect she has on them.

"The steps of a good man [or woman] are ordered by the Lord" (Ps. 37:23). Those steps are so designed by Him to influence every person within the reach of the atmosphere she sets.

Are you setting a good or bad atmosphere by your sweet or sour spirit? Do people associate these words with the aura that surrounds you: cheer, happiness, gladness, beauty, strength, fun, excitement, love, purity, peace, joy, gentleness, kindness and goodness?

"But the fruit of the Spirit is love, joy, peace, longsuffering, gentleness, goodness, faith, Meekness, temperance: against such there is no law" (Gal. 5:22,23).

Are you a wounded spirit, associated with blackness and gossip ("The words of a talebearer are as wounds, and they go down into the innermost parts of the belly"—Prov. 18:8); hatred, strife, wrath ("He that is slow to wrath is of great understanding. . ." —Prov. 14:29); nagging, envy and heaviness ("Heaviness in the heart of man maketh it stoop: but a good word maketh it glad"—Prov. 12:25)? Do you hate reproof and refuse instruction ("He that refuseth instruction despiseth his own soul: but he that heareth reproof getteth understanding"—Prov. 15:32)?

The Atmosphere Extends to a Height of 22,000 Miles!

This fact is astounding, but I'm not unduly impressed because

I've seen the atmosphere a woman sets extend so shockingly far that I have no doubt about its reaching 22,000 years into the future. (Forgive me for not understanding eternity's timetable.)

"And I heard a voice from heaven saying unto me, Write, Blessed are the dead which die in the Lord from henceforth: Yea, saith the Spirit, that they may rest from their labours; and their works do follow them" (Rev. 14:13).

Without even thinking twice on the subject or pulling certain letters on purpose, I just happen to have some paragraphs from letters in the to-be-answered stack by my side which are thrilling examples of the extent of our influence through the atmosphere we create.

A young lady from Lancaster, South Carolina, writes:

> I heard something one of your Hyles-Anderson College girls said to a friend who visited there recently, and I want to be able to say the same thing and mean it with all my heart. The girl said that she didn't want to talk about anything other than the Lord and His goodness. I cannot say that I am as sure of my motives, but I think I truly want to be consumed and constrained by the love of Christ. I want to go to Hyles-Anderson College if it will help me to be what the Lord has intended.

What part do you suppose a passing remark from that college girl will have on the life of a twenty-three-year-old girl who now wants God's best for her life? What influence will this young lady from South Carolina have on someone someday? What if that girl had been giving off a "gripey" remark, maybe something she did not even mean? Could someone or maybe hundreds of someones have been affected throughout years to come? I don't know, but the thought is scary!

Let me pick up a card written by Nola DuBois, a graduate of Hyles-Anderson, about Carol Frye, a dormitory supervisor:

> The love and care Miss Frye has given me overwhelms me and seems to run over. It causes me to love her more, love God more, love others more and even think more of myself. Without her, I would never have known I could be an influence used of God to help change the lives of others. It seems impossible

> that she is now sending girls to me for help. She builds me, which gives me the confidence to try to soak up teaching enough to be able to help someone else.

Then, I pick up a thank-you letter from Carol to me in which she kindly encourages me with:

> So much of my thinking was wrong, and I didn't even know it. It has taken a lot of teaching and many years of hard work on your part to train that out of me. To me it sure was and is worth all that you have taught me; only eternity will tell what your relationship to me will mean to others.

Of course, anything I've given her comes from parents, aunts and uncles, preachers, Sunday school teachers and friends.

Where will it all end? At a height of 22,000 miles? Never! You see, I'm more impressed with the spiritual atmosphere He has created through us than with that of the scientific world.

The Atmosphere Rotates With the Earth!

The atmosphere is the supporting element to the earth, just as wives are the supporting element to husbands.

I was planning to talk to girls and women on this subject at Youth Conference one year when I saw a pastor from out west. I was relating to him my thoughts concerning women and atmosphere when he broke into smiles, saying, "Yes, my wife is as a sweet breath of fresh air." Then he really got into it and told me that the sweet atmosphere which permeates the surroundings of his wife transmits and reflects the Son, just as the scientific atmosphere transmits and reflects the sun.

I feel that is as it should be since, "Ye are the light of the world. A city that is set on an hill cannot be hid. Let your light so shine before men, that they may see your good works, and glorify your Father which is in heaven" (Matt. 5:14,16).

The Atmosphere Permeates!

The atmosphere pervades, permeates and saturates like water soaks through a sponge. It surrounds as a general mood our social environment or tone. A great deal of concern over pollution has been in evidence for years, but little has been done to fight the horrible ugly tongues of vocal pollution which spew out of our mouths regularly.

The other day I was sitting in a position where I couldn't help but observe a family ordering their meals. I overheard the mother say, "Hurry up! She's waiting! Don't take all day!" Her face was cold and hard as she hatefully looked in the direction of her small son.

I asked myself how many times had I acted the same way because of false pride. We sometimes allow embarrassment to cause us to hurt our own children with whom we live, rather than risk a sour look from a waitress whom we'll never see again. Usually a child's hesitation in such a situation is our fault because of a lack of training, and I guess our guilt is the source of the ugliness we dispense.

As I watched this particular display, it reminded me of snake venom, for the whole family sat in a "blue funk" for the remainder of their time in the restaurant. I believe they were poisoned by words, don't you?

Our words do a lot to set the atmosphere which surrounds us. Every word we say either goes forth to bless, or to curse and wound. The following verses show the importance of our words:

"A man hath joy by the answer of his mouth: and a word spoken in due season, how good is it!" (Prov. 15:23).

"A word fitly spoken is like apples of gold in pictures of silver" (Prov. 25:11).

"She openeth her mouth with wisdom; and in her tongue is the law of kindness" (Prov. 31:26).

The really diabolical thing about using words in a wrong way is that our vocal tone, countenance and body motions are audio-visual equipment used to cut those words into the heart of another very effectively.

I used to hear Dr. Lee Roberson discuss liberalism and other equally bad "isms" in terms of being *pusillanimous.* I wasn't sure of the meaning of the word, but I got the idea that it was not good. The dictionary confirmed my belief. It seems to be a good adjective to use concerning gripey, complaining, jealous and harsh words.

I only wish there were some way for me to realize how utterly abominable my negative remarks sound. In an effort to know how bad I can sound, I try to think of all the gross and horrendous things on which we do not wish to think—pus, mucus and vomit, to name a few. My mind even wanders to the odor given off by a skunk as I think of those words or facial expressions expressed by teenagers as "bad vibes."

The most discordant note in music cannot grate against our flesh or cause our skin to crawl as much as a hateful or sarcastic word can. Hatefulness seems to go with haughtiness, about which Isaiah speaks: "Moreover the Lord saith, Because the daughters of Zion are haughty, and walk with stretched forth necks and wanton eyes, walking and mincing as they go..." (Isa. 3:16).

Then Isaiah 3:24 tells us: "And it shall come to pass, that instead of sweet smell there shall be stink; and instead of a girdle a rent; and instead of well set hair baldness; and instead of a stomacher a girding of sackcloth; and burning instead of beauty."

Yes, stink, rent, baldness, sackcloth and burning seem to approach somewhat the horrible, asinine, hateful, spiteful ways we Christian women too often exhibit.

A bad atmosphere is as stifling to God's will as a high ozone level is to breathing. So let's turn off the snide, putrid remarks we're so quick to spit out.

An Atmosphere Has an Interesting Effect

This meaning given in the dictionary is somewhat different from the others which pertained to the scientific atmosphere:

An atmosphere is an interesting, often exotic, effect produced by decoration and furnishings.

Have you ever read those stories which feature a girl preparing her home or apartment in a way that would appeal to her boy friend? Perhaps you've heard a girl discussing her plans for such an event. This usually includes steak, candles, soft music, low lights, perfume and pretty clothes.

This is a deadly combination which can be used in a dangerously wrong way or in a wonderfully right way. (As usual, we're all mixed up; we create the right atmosphere at the wrong time. How long after marriage do the candlelight dinners take place?) This atmosphere gets to you through five senses: perfume and steak—sense of smell; candlelight and appropriate table—sense of sight; music—sense of hearing; steak—sense of taste; and, of course, all of these naturally lead to the sense of touch.

Wouldn't it be great if we waited to perform these or similar rites after marriage rather than before marriage? It doesn't take two people to set an atmosphere. You can be the atmosphere setter!

Homes have an atmosphere . . . schools and classrooms within schools have an atmosphere . . . and churches have an atmosphere. There are disorderly, unclean, unorganized homes which regularly dispatch unorganized and disorderly family members into the world. However, there are also homes which produce orderly minds and self-confident individuals who believe they are loved and can face the world with a healthy sense of humor. Truly, these people are a reflection of the leadership of their homes. Atmosphere does make a difference!

Some churches are known for their friendliness and others for their coldness. It's an atmosphere set by the leaders. Women can help their leaders make a friendly church. However, I warn you that you will have to sacrifice if you want to participate in "Operation Friendly Church." You will have to give up your friends! That's right! The cliques will have to go!

So many people exclaim over their friendly churches, when I have found them to be the opposite. They think they are friendly because about everyone will go to the newcomers and say, "Hi, how are you? I hope you come back soon." I call these people the "hit-and-run" type. As soon as they have made their "duty call," they run back to their "security blanket" (the people by whom they've been sitting for twenty years).

Now, come on! I know we love to be with our friends, but couldn't we bring a newcomer to sit with our gang? Even better, just once in awhile, we could leave the group or special friend, saying, "I'm going to sit with that new lady. See you after church so we can ride home together."

You see, best friends and cliques are going to see to it that they get together; we must make a way on purpose to include others. Supposedly friendly churches sometimes close ranks to the point that a visitor begins to feel there is no way to "crack the group."

Try examining your church for friendliness from the viewpoint of a visitor. What is the true A.Q. (Atmosphere Quotient)? A woman could set the pace and by doing so, show her love for the Lord, her help to the preacher and her concern for the stranger. "When saw we thee a stranger, and took thee in?" (Matt. 25:38).

My Sunday school teacher, Mrs. Olin Holbrook, was a widow for fourteen years before she remarried. During those years she had one of those beautiful, special relationships with another widow lady whom she had known most of her life. I admired Mrs. Holbrook and Mrs. Elinore Hawkins because their friendship was never exclusive. Many times they rode together to and from an event, but they went their separate ways and toward others during the actual time of the occasion.

Best friends are going to be close without a lot of on-purpose planning, but getting to know new people will probably take some real thought, and perhaps effort, on our parts.

Our preacher tells dating couples that they should gather from many outside their twosome in order to keep their relationship alive and well. It is so true that exclusivism is excludism and cannot bring blessing to any relationship in any way.

What Your Heart Ponders, Your Face Reveals!

"For Jerusalem is ruined, and Judah is fallen: because their tongue and their doings are against the Lord, to provoke the eyes of his glory. The shew of their countenance doth witness against them" (Isa. 3:8,9).

When we made faces as little kids, people told us our faces would freeze that way. There is more truth than fiction in this, for we see mature people whose faces are set into upward happy lines or downward ugly lines.

This is how we can set the atmosphere for happy lines in our faces: "Let the words of my mouth, and the meditation of my heart, be acceptable in thy sight, O Lord, my strength, and my redeemer" (Ps. 19:14).

17 – Control That Temperament!

EXTRA! EXTRA! Read all about it! I have good news for you. You don't have to stay the way you are!

Now, don't let me upset you in any way; if you want to stay the way you are, please feel free. I just know I don't want to die with the same faults. Okay?

Matthew 5:6 says, "Blessed are they which do hunger and thirst after righteousness: for they shall be filled." In my thinking, this is one of the greatest promises in the Bible. The burden is placed squarely on us. If we want it, we can have it. Most women do get just about what they set out to get, if they really truly want it.

Once upon a time when I sold china, crystal and silver in direct sales work, I was taught to recognize the fact that women could and would buy what they really wanted. The sales manuals placed the blame for failure to make a sale on the salesperson. "If she does not buy, it is because you have not sold. You have not done a piece of sales work which created desire enough to overcome all objections."

Until then, I always thought people did not buy because they could not afford it, didn't need it, husband wouldn't let them, or they had no place to display, use or store it. I found that a woman who really wanted china would rationalize any or all of these supposed reasons for not buying, completely into oblivion. Believe me, I'm not saying this is right; I am saying, for the most part, it is true.

If this is true to any degree, then why are we not finding ways to love people, win souls, keep house, learn good grooming, excel in child training, lose weight, memorize the Bible, and a million and one other things that we say we really want?

You Can Add to Your Life!

I hate to admit this, but it must be that we do not actually want it. I have never taken logic nor have I ever been accused of being overly logical, but I surely must have a logical thesis here.

Let's take Bible memorization, for instance. Oh, I am sure most of us would be receptive to the idea of God's pouring 500 new verses into our brains as a direct result of prayer; therefore, we say we would really like to know more Bible. The truth is, we like newspaper, television, books and magazines more than we do the Bible. Yes, we would like to know the Bible, but we do not hunger and thirst to know it.

Let's look at another decoy—soul winning. Do you long to see souls saved as a result of your telling the old, old story? "For he satisfieth the longing soul, and filleth the hungry soul with goodness" (Ps. 107:9). "The young lions do lack, and suffer hunger: but they that seek the Lord shall not want any good thing" (Ps. 34:10). If we are not filled and are still wanting this good thing (souls saved), we must not be honestly seeking the Lord.

I can remember going forward several times to a church altar, saying, "Lord, this sermon has convicted me about soul winning; I have to win souls or die." I really meant it at the altar, but I did not long for it enough to find a soul winner who would take me out and train me. I would just try on my own, make a few people mad, get some doors slammed in my face and give up again.

Then the next time I heard a good soul-winning sermon or experienced the death of an unsaved acquaintance, I went to the altar again. I would read a soul-winning course or book which did not take me where the action was (among people where souls were being won), and I would fail again.

I am glad I had sense enough to keep making public my desire to win souls even if I did not do anything about it. Sometimes we are foolish enough to tell ourselves to forget it forever. It does hurt our pride, doesn't it? Maybe a little smarting of false pride will finally spur us on to seek the face of God until we find the answer.

Stay Around People You Do Not Like!

Not knowing what you want in life, I still know one direction in which to point you. You, however, probably won't like it. STAY AROUND PEOPLE WHO HAVE WHAT YOU DO NOT HAVE.

The reason this may be painful is caused by the fact that people who have strengths you lack, may have temperaments you have not learned to understand. The philosophy, "If you don't like 'em, leave 'em," makes for very little growth caught from other people. Learn to love those you do not like, and God will add to your likes.

One time a new Hyles-Anderson student wife showed up in a Christian Womanhood class. When I asked each one to tell what she wanted to gain from taking the course, the new girl replied, "I don't even want to be here. It costs money we don't have. I won't learn anything anyway. My husband will soon be starting a job, which will mean I won't have a babysitter or a way to get here. It's such a waste!"

Now, you will have to admit that remarks such as these before a group of thirty ladies would not cause you to be automatically attracted to the person who was the source of such "blasphemy." Does the Bible say, "Love those who are nice to you, speak all manner of good about you, and like you"? Of course not! No one has to tell us to love that kind. We just naturally love them because it is usually easy to do so. Please read Matthew 5:43-48:

"Ye have heard that it hath been said, Thou shalt love thy neighbour, and hate thine enemy. But I say unto you, Love your enemies, bless them that curse you, do good to them that hate you, and pray for them which despitefully use you, and persecute you; That ye may be the children of your Father which is in heaven: for he maketh his sun to rise on the evil and on the good, and sendeth rain on the just and on the unjust. For if ye love them which love you, what reward have ye? do not even the publicans the same? And if ye salute your brethren only, what do ye more than others? do not even the publicans so? Be ye therefore perfect, even as your Father which is in heaven is perfect."

Let's specifically look at part of verse 46: "For if ye love them which love you, what reward have ye? do not even the publicans the same?" True love is not given or withheld because of actions, for it is unconditional.

Brother Hyles says love does not depend on the condition of the recipient but on the condition of the one who loves. The only way we are able to give true love is through the grace of God, for "God is love" (I John 4:8).

Oh, I forgot to tell you about the girl. She and I talked a long time after class that night—long enough for me to discover the real problem. She felt she could never be a lady, and she was scared to death by the fact that her husband felt called to Christian work. She just knew she could not be a preacher's wife.

How I have thanked God I did not get hostile or mentally throw her out! She has become just as outgoing in service as she used to be verbally. She probably has helped me much more than I ever will be able to help her.

Go ahead! Love those to whom you are naturally drawn, but be sure you add to your life by learning to love those you do not like!

Do Things You Don't Like to Do

Go against your feelings! You realize I do not mean you should do anything which would hurt your testimony for Christ. I am afraid most of the things we won't do have to do with our selfishness, laziness and self will, instead of our testimony!

How often do you hear Christian women say, "Oh, I couldn't do that!" in reference to something they have never tried or in connection with a situation they feel they can't face? It is true that some of this temperament control is impossible with people, ". . . but with God all things are possible" (Matt. 19:26).

Be careful that you don't try to become someone else. You can't really change yourself; the Holy Spirit is the One who can change you. "Therefore if any man be in Christ, he is a new creature: old things are passed away; behold, all things are become new" (II Cor. 5:17). Even then, you were made by God to be you, and He wants to use your strengths for His own purposes, which will eventually bring you good.

Until you accept what you cannot change, you will probably not see that which is changeable changed. Accepting ourselves as God wants us takes Philippians 4:13: "I can do all things through Christ which strengtheneth me."

If you are a quiet, reserved person who enjoys staying home most of the time, preferring to see people as little as possible, and you are really proficient in sewing, needlepoint, reading and writing, it is doubtful that you ought to change in order to become a nationwide speaker. But wouldn't it be something to become tempered to the point that you could add to your life by teaching a small group of girls and discipling one or more of them? Go ahead with your office work, sewing or reading—we need you for every strength you have—but enrichment means adding.

Recently a lovely Christian lady said, "I've always been a Martha; but now that I'm adding some Mary, I'm enjoying it." I know she'll stay a Martha—she's such a needed one—but I'm going to watch for a thrill as she adds a touch of Mary and as she lets God do an exciting work in her.

One time while several of us were working with a college girl—a Martha trying to add Mary—I think we just about let her choke to death on Mary. She worked all day long on Mary projects which she couldn't quite handle. This caused her to feel she was one big mistake. This young lady is a fantastic Martha and is tremendously used of God in that capacity.

We hurriedly guided her back to 75% Martha tasks and counseled her to add Mary jobs in smaller doses.

I wonder why Mary couldn't have exchanged places with Martha just long enough to watch the biscuits in order for Martha to sit at Jesus' feet a few minutes.

Do you wonder if Mary felt she was too good to do kitchen work? Do you think Martha felt too intimidated to leave the security of the kitchen—a place where she felt competent? Do you suppose Mary was so absorbed and engrossed in what she was doing that it never occurred to her to offer to help Martha?

I wonder if Martha didn't like to have anyone in her kitchen. Maybe Mary felt it was her mission in life to entertain everyone (always on stage). Would you think Martha liked to do all the work, feel persecuted and remind everyone of her martyrdom? Did you ever wonder if Mary really loved Jesus more than Martha did? Did Martha really feel that caring for Jesus physically was showing more love?

I can never figure out these things, can you? About the time I'm all "up in arms" about some folks doing wrong in some of these ways, I find they're all upset about it themselves. Since they don't know what is right, they hide their real feelings; so no one can help them.

If there is someone you want to criticize, try to discover what her thinking could be. Give her the benefit of the doubt so you can help her in love.

Is there someone whose actions you're always trying to defend—daughter, mother or best friend? Let's jump on the band-wagon of the mind to give every person the same benefit. Wouldn't the world be something if, to ourselves, we mentally defended everyone? This would make it possible to love people to us so we could help them. When that happens, we usually find that the problems of others are completely different from what we had thought.

Do you say you don't want to do that? Do it anyway. It will add to their lives—and to yours!

Get Help!

It's so tragic when we act as if we're wary animals in a jungle jockeying for position and therefore unable ever to show any weakness in any way. It is sad, because we get worse as we save face in "hiding our faults" by not getting help. If we aren't on them "like a chicken on a June bug," faults and weaknesses have a way of overwhelming us in a manner that definitely cannot be hidden.

Now I don't mean you should go from house to house proclaiming yourself a disaster area. Two things are wrong with that type conduct. First, almost everyone will give you unneeded sympathy and conflicting advice, and then go to someone else to discuss with them your problem. It is a poisonous form of self-indulgence to have everyone discussing you. Second, you should declare yourself off limits to human beings or unfit for human fellowship for one area of life when you're in the midst of a hurricane. Just survive the season, then go to just one person who has strengths in your weak areas. Or you might not even want to discuss with another what you're doing, as long as you have faced it yourself.

I know what you're going to ask: "What if I do talk to someone and find that she tells other people?" Just count on that happening, because I can assure you it will—sometime. Well-meaning people are still human. Accepting that fact will give you great peace about the failures and foibles of your brothers and sisters in Christ.

Knowing this better than we could ever comprehend it, God still placed the burden of soul winning and witnessing on His people! We fail Him all the time, but He helps us up once again and then goes on depending on us. This truth should keep us from puzzling over the faults of man.

Man isn't much, but God counts on him. God tells us, "Confess your faults one to another, and pray one for another, that ye may be healed. The effectual fervent prayer of a righteous man availeth much" (James 5:16). And, "Bear ye one another's burdens, and so fulfill the law of Christ" (Gal. 6:2).

We must go ahead trusting and loving the Word of God so that we can still have peace when betrayed. "Great peace have they which love thy law: and nothing shall offend them" (Ps. 119:165).

It really is true that we get upset with people in direct proportion to how much we love and learn the Bible. OUCH!

Balance Eludes Us

How often we have said, "I just can't get the right balance on that thing in my life."

Yes, we get one area going well and another goes "kaflooey." It must be a horrendous thing to keep three circus rings going well. We can ask God to make us friendly; then we fall overboard being silly, giggly, slaphappy idiots! Sometimes the pendulum swings to extremes before we can learn, "Let your moderation be known unto all men. The Lord is at hand" (Phil. 4:5). When we go to the extreme, we sometimes are tempted to give up and not go to God for added help. Going to extremes is a trick the devil uses to keep us from becoming balanced people whom God can use.

Circus people spend many hours practicing in order to thrill us with their balance.

One summer the kids and I went to Marriot's Great America, a theme park in Illinois up close to the Wisconsin line. A feature provided by the park was a miniature circus.

Knowing that the program did not start for a couple of hours, we were surprised, when we walked by, to detect noise and action going on above the ground. Our questioning brought out the fact that they practice all day long, even though they perform just four times a day. Yes, those people went through all that to get balance on unicycles, trampolines, swings, ropes and bars.

Young children spend hours learning to ride their bicycles with "no hands."

Those who water-ski torture their muscles before they begin to get that balance which makes for a sport of grace and beauty.

Models support books on their heads as they walk (for several hours each day for many months) in order to capture that elusive thing called balance.

Balance attracts us, even captivates us to the point that we are fascinated by animals that learn to balance balls while standing on stools. We drive far to see huge, balanced rocks. I suppose, as in all else, we are captivated by that which we do not have. Balance is no doubt one of the most difficult characteristics to acquire in life. No wonder Dr. Hyles' books, *Blue Denim and Lace, Grace and Truth* and *Strength and Beauty* are loved so well!

"And Jesus increased in wisdom and stature, and in favour with God and man" (Luke 2:52). If Jesus grew mentally, physically, spiritually and socially, we have a pretty good Example for going on to perfection (maturity).

Let's become mature people as we develop a balanced life. The Word of God is a balanced Book, and it can make you a balanced person. The book of Proverbs is the greatest psychology book in the world. It shows us how to understand ourselves and others. What better psychology than, "Withdraw thy foot from thy neighbour's house; lest he be weary of thee, and so hate thee" (Prov. 25:17). That means you shouldn't spend time gossiping when you drop by to leave the cookies for vacation Bible school! At least, that's what it means to me.

Go to the balanced Book to learn about the balanced Jesus who will point you to balanced people in order for you to be a balanced person He can use.

18 – I See Gold Glittering There!

Why do Sunday school teachers, bus workers and Bible club leaders quit to go into activities which are eventually so much less rewarding and fulfilling?

Perhaps the key to the answer is in the word *eventually.* We just can't wait for the end result, the last chapter, or see things in light of the "long haul."

The other day I was asked, "What about all the people you help who don't turn out right?" I answered the question with, "Are they dead yet?" The girl shook her head no. Then I questioned, "How do you know they aren't going to turn out right?" Unless they are dead, you don't know; then, you can't really know whether or not you've helped them even in their dying hours.

Our problem isn't that there aren't enough good results from seed we've sown but immaturity which causes us to seek immediate solutions and keeps us from waiting for the end results.

True, there is little or no immediate glamor or recognition in helping a class of wiggly second graders. Sometimes there's not even much excitement or sense of achievement; and certainly there's no thought of advancement or money.

My brother-in-law was a principal of a school in a big city educational system before he left that work to go into Christian education. He started a Christian school that became very successful. People knew of the work of Jerry Smith because his displays and projects were very well received at Christian educational seminars and conferences. His school was organized and produced results which caused it to grow.

For many years he has been teaching future schoolteachers and administrators who are training at Hyles-Anderson College. He is also a Sunday school teacher of second-grade boys who come to the First Baptist Church of Hammond, Indiana, from East Chicago and Chicago-type areas.

He really worked hard to get control over a particular class of unruly boys and then did his best to see growth in the number of boys being reached. One week he made calls, visited in homes and sent forty handwritten cards, only to find that his attendance went down the very next Sunday.

Have you ever seen that happen? Has that ever happened to you? Did you use it as an excuse to give up? No, no, no! Never give up for such a reason. Find something to grasp onto as you decide that the work will pay off—"over the long haul."

Jerry took comfort and received satisfaction that day when one little ragged urchin came to Sunday school with his card clutched firmly against him. It was obvious that he had read and reread it as he carried it wherever he went.

Find something like that and dwell on it, talk about it, build it in your mind and tell yourself that one little boy probably received the only piece of mail he's ever had come to him in his very own name. Take that thought apart; chew on it. Talk to yourself some more and say, *That little boy may now think more of himself because God used me to send him a card. I wonder if he saw his name in a different light because of someone's caring to write to him. Could this incident, which seems so little to me, influence him for good sometime even later in his life?*

Force yourself to remember just such occasions from your own young life which have never left you. If you will make a big deal out of it, you'll not be discouraged to the point of wanting to change to a "better" work. Make the work you have better by altering it "over the long haul."

Had Jerry Smith not seen gold glittering in one little boy and had he not seen gold glittering in one little act, he probably would have been on the depressed list, too. It would have been very easy for Jerry to become disheartened had he thought only of past jobs he had performed and compared that to this one day in Sunday school. But he got his ego-building from God, who let him see one little boy and one little card.

We all need to know that we are achievers, that we're admired, loved and honored. But don't expect these needs to be met by people. God alone can see to it that you enjoy these things on your own if you will trust Him.

Are you a seamstress? Do you know one? I've never known one who preferred to alter clothes. Most women who are good with the needle want to create and want to start from the beginning. It is not as exciting to take in, let out and adjust. Who knows what you've done? No one comes up to ask, "Who altered your dress?" They will admiringly ask, "Did you make that?"

Just as it is less exciting to alter clothes, it is less exciting to alter the situation of a Sunday school class. You are tempted to begin all over again. New beginnings are more exciting. Don't yield to this temptation, or you might be one to give up relationships (such as a job or a marriage), thinking it more fun to start anew.

A husband who runs to someone he isn't married to may find fun and excitement for awhile–fun and excitement that could have come from altering the relationship he already had with his wife. And his wife could make him happier over "the long haul."

Learn to stay by Sunday school classes, jobs and relationships you have with friends and relatives. Look for gold glittering where you have not seen it before.

"They Just Ain't Seen No Gold Yet!"

That's right! When you quit, it's because "you just ain't seen no gold yet!"

Remember the stories of the gold rush? People waited for as long as it took to find gold. Just about the time they had decided to give up and go home, they would see a little streak of yellow, so they would begin again with renewed vigor.

Sometimes it's difficult to see real gold in those bus kids; but if you dwell on them long enough, you'll see gold glittering there. As long as you can keep your eyes on that little glitter, you stand a good chance of being there when the gold comes in.

And I'm here to tell you that it does come in. In some cases you wait for years, but you also find cases where you can't believe the quality of the gold when it does begin to come through. Even you people-developers who dream dreams other people didn't fathom, sometimes realize there are those who go far beyond your fondest dreams.

Don't give up! You think you're no good? You say no one lets you know they've reaped from what you've sown? Evaluation of a person who works with people, whether it be in Sunday school, training union, bus work or in your own home, takes years, just as it takes years to evaluate a President of the United States.

I know how you feel. Sometimes the one who seems to be the weakest teacher in school or Sunday school seems to be the most popular. I remember the teacher of young people who spent most of every Sunday school hour letting the pupils talk about what they did the night before, with no applications given. I recall how she told them Sunday after Sunday that she was not prepared, for she had had a busy week. Yet she was popular, for she would listen to the young people as they sat and talked and laughed about worldly activities in which they were engaged.

Feel sorry for her, yes—but don't be jealous of her popularity. Be concerned for her and the young people, yes—but go on doing right and making right as attractive as possible. The last chapter isn't in yet!

Because children, youths and childish people of all ages usually do not have or understand eternal values, you may not be popular if you teach with eternity's values in view. But as these same children or childish adults gain spiritual insight, you will become more popular with them. By that time, popularity will not even matter as you begin to grow into the maturity of teaching for "long-haul" growth.

Time-Released Teaching!

Don't worry if certain people you try to help don't seem to like your method of teaching: they may get the full force of it someday when they need it.

One time when I visited with Annie Ruth McGuire, a friend in Chattanooga, Tennessee. She kept taking time-released capsules for a bronchial condition. When I learned that some of the medicine was released immediately, while other portions were stored in the body until needed, I immediately recognized that this was the story of my own teaching.

I don't know how many letters we receive saying to the effect that this particular person didn't know what she had gotten from me at a meeting where I had taught, until a need arose weeks or months later. Students often tell me they did not understand my college classes until they got out and faced a problem. Then the teaching came in on them. Read the following example:

> I am constantly amazed at the practical teaching which you have given. At first I thought it "rinky-dink," if you'll excuse me, but soon I began to see your teaching in action! All the time your lectures keep coming to my mind and they help me to deal with both personal situations and situations involving others.

Following one of our first Spectaculars (which *Christian Womanhood* sponsors annually at the First Baptist Church of Hammond, Indiana), a lady wrote:

> I heard of your meeting and was having marriage problems. I brought several ladies to the Spectacular from New York at great sacrifice. We thought we were going to get something. I was disappointed Friday afternoon, but thought maybe I'd get it that night. After that night, I thought maybe I was too tired and would get something Saturday. I didn't get it Saturday. I went home very discouraged.
>
> Then a week later when our family got into the car to go to church, my husband and I started our usual bickering. Then I found out what I had gotten at the Spectacular! Something strange happened. I couldn't bicker!
>
> At the time of the writing of this letter six months have passed: I still can't bicker! I don't know how it happened or at what point I got it. I can't remember who taught it. I just know I got it!

This is a prime example of time-released teaching. It sometimes comes as a result of telling personal stories, "entertaining" to keep folks awake, and placing many people before the audience in order to relate to all different kinds of personalities. If you do these things, people might critically accuse you of being shallow. Yet they are the very makings of causing deep decisions about real-life matters.

Sunday school teachers, if you're having results, don't quit your method. Be sure you're teaching within the boundary of the Word of God and counseling with godly people, but forget the destructive criticism. Children and young people have opinions, and they believe that the democratic system gives them the right to express these opinions. They don't have the discernment to know that there are teachers who teach, those who touch, and those who do both. If they could discern this, they would know to get all they can from all three kinds and hold their negative opinions to themselves.

I once had a teacher who seemingly didn't touch; she only taught. She was a spinster lady (truly in characteristics as well as marital status) who had the misfortune of being placed over a bunch of six or eight young teenagers at a Youth Fellowship in Blue Springs, Nebraska.

We chewed her up and spit her out in little pieces. Bless her heart! She was a friend of my mother, and a good woman—one who was only filling in because there was no one else and because she had been asked to help. She gave us facts, but apparently didn't touch our lives. This was not because her heart wasn't in it. It was because she didn't know our age group or type, and no one helped her. (I think teachers who just teach give facts from the head. They at least lead from the head. Teachers who touch lead with the heart.) Though she didn't know how to lead with the heart, yet God blessed her willingness.

She asked to see me one night after Youth Fellowship. We had "cut up" and talked very badly that night. With tears in her eyes, she said, "Marlene, I guess I'm not too surprised at the other kids, but I thought you'd be different."

The fact that I've recalled that scene hundreds of times and am still doing so means she did touch my life! Perhaps something you do will touch a life even though you (and others) feel you only give facts.

There are scores of ways to teach. I've learned so much from a couple of phrases my friend, Nancy Perry, from Hendersonville, North Carolina, uses repeatedly. When I ask, "Nancy, isn't it hard to see your little grandson running around and not have your husband Paul here to see and enjoy him?" she always answers that type of question with, "If I let myself think about it," or, "I'm not going to worry about it." She teaches by common sense (which, by the way, is in great demand these days).

Dr. Bob Jones, Sr., taught by repetition, and some of those who criticized him for doing it are now out spouting the very truths he taught and retaught.

"For precept must be upon precept, precept upon precept; line upon line, line upon line; here a little, and there a little" (Isa. 28:10).

My seventh-grade teacher, Mrs. Thoman, taught through kindness. You all don't know that your reading material was written by the third-place winner of the Gage County (Beatrice, Nebraska) spelling contest, do you? I was so enthralled with the distinguished honor that I felt I shouldn't have to take any more spelling tests the rest of the year since I was so far above the other mere mortals in my class! So, I told my mom something to that effect.

Evidently my dear mother told Mrs. Thoman how nice it was that I didn't have to take those spelling tests, because Mrs. Thoman came by my desk, leaned over and quietly said, "Marlene, why don't you go ahead and take each of the spelling tests this year just to firm the sets of words in your mind?" She knew and I knew what had happened, but she saved face for me. I knew I'd done wrong. She taught me through kindness. Some would have criticized her for not "getting me" directly.

Most of what I have learned best is that which has come through the heart. If you lead with the mind, you can reach only those whose minds travel on your same wave length. But if you lead with the mind and heart, you can touch everyone because of the universal need for hearts to reach hearts.

However, do your best at what you can do at this time in your life, and don't quit!

You Should See Gold Where No One Else Suspects It!

Some people see gold in only certain types of people. They say, "That's my type of person." Well, if that's your only type, those will be the only ones you can teach or touch. You'd better start looking for gold where you or others might least expect it.

Some folks never have a ghost of an idea that there is any gold. They say, "Everybody's out for himself." Maybe to a point this is true. However, considering the depravity of man, wouldn't it be fun to be in on the developing of people? You could have a part in the little bit they are doing right when they do begin to have periods of living Christlike lives.

Still others believe there's gold, but they don't know how to go about digging for it. They can't see it before it's there in all its glory. That means they can't be people-developers—real teachers.

In my orthopedically handicapped class was a little seven-year-old girl with cerebral palsy. Since she had come from a pre-school where the children had called the teachers by their last names, she called me "Ebans," not being able to pronounce the "v" in Evans. She'd call, "Ebans," and I would say, "Mrs. Evans, Janie." This went on all year, but I might as well have "joined 'em" because I couldn't "lick 'em." She often forgot her words when I had her read, and she'd say, "It not matter, Ebans." That phrase became a regular part of my talking to myself.

Perhaps Janie shouldn't have taken that attitude about reading. However, maybe she knew, "It not matter, Ebans," because she died a year later. I saw some gold in her and learned from her as I valued her life, for even now when I get all harried I say, "It not matter, Ebans." And it usually doesn't!!

Billy and Benny McCrary were in our church in Hendersonville, North Carolina, when my husband was a young pastor there. At that time they were young teenagers. One weighed a little over 300 pounds, and the other weighed a little under that!

They came to youth meetings at our house and saw my husband's *Matthew Henry Commentaries*; they began to study them and would present programs reading from them.

Later, Billy and Benny were named the world's largest twins and were written up in the *GUINNESS BOOK OF WORLD RECORDS*. They were on the Merv Griffin Show, they were featured on a page of LIFE magazine, and they also went into rodeos with some kind of an act.

As I read about them, I often wondered if they remembered anything we taught them. We saw gold there. I wonder if we were wrong. One died at an early age, and the other now weighs over 700 pounds. Newspaper articles tell me he won't live very long. I don't know what will happen to him, but I refuse to believe we were wrong. The last chapter is not in yet!

In that same church was a girl named Kathy Morgan. She would often call me after school to tell me all that went on in the halls of Hendersonville High School that day. She would question me and use me as a sounding board when she'd say, "I don't see anything wrong with dancing." There were those who took this seeming brazenness to be that of a girl who would never be anything. Really she was just making the statements in order to get reassurance and find answers to what her unsaved friends were asking her.

The last chapter is not in on Kathy yet; but, as of now, she has worked with and helped dozens of teenagers in the Hendersonville, North Carolina, area and is married to a fine Christian preacher.

Why Do I See Gold Glittering There?

I see gold glittering in young people because Mom and Dad saw gold glittering in me. In fact, I once told my dad it was all his fault when I became very disheartened with a number of people with whom I was working. It seemed as though their glitter was never going to shine brightly and that they were going to take me down with them. I said, "Dad, if you hadn't put up with me and some of my antics, I wouldn't be feeling as though I had to put up with everybody else."

One time my dad told me I could go to the drugstore and charge on his bill if I really had to have something while Mom was in the hospital. I took this as a license to take all my friends (and I seemed to gain many at that time) by the drugstore several times a day in order to purchase "necessary" items such as ice cream cones, candy bars and gum.

Dad was very shocked when he received his monthly statement so littered by my "emergency" items. However, as well as I can remember, he didn't threaten me with reform school (even if there was a girls' reformatory close by in Geneva, Nebraska). Neither did he stand and wring his hands over the prospect of my ending up in the state penitentiary which was close by in Lincoln.

Instead, he did something very practical. He insisted I start my career at the ripe old age of ten or eleven. He and Mom looked over the *Grit* newspaper advertisements and found I could order general cards to peddle door to door.

As I sold sympathy, get well and baby cards, I made my weekly payment for my "emergency" bill at the drugstore. What could have been a very bad scene ended up helping me to face things as I learned how to handle wrong done in my life.

Because they saw gold in me, I learned that God saw gold in me. In fact, He made any that is in me. "Every good gift and every perfect gift is from above" (James 1:17). He knows where it is. He understands and is patient when the little bit of gold doesn't show. Are you?

19 – Correction

"Oh, but Susie doesn't know how to correct. That's why Jane is so upset."

"You can't tell Mary anything. She never can take suggestions."

Personally, I'm so sad every time I hear one of the above statements—or one similar to them—that I just have to talk a bit about the need of knowing how to give or take correction.

When you get right down to it, who does know how to do either? I'm sure I certainly lack finesse in both areas. There is a real art to the skill of correcting in such a way that it gives permanent help instead of permanent hurt. Notice, I used the word *permanent.* Correction can seldom be taken without at least temporary hurt. The important thing is, "What will it do for a person over the long haul?"

You may ask, "Why are you so sad about this subject?" I believe the lack of knowledge in how to handle the area of correction (give or take) in our lives is also the reason for lack of growth in our lives. It is the reason we go to our graves with the same weaknesses (uncontrolled) and faults of a lifetime.

Of course, the Word of God could correct us on its own, but God chose to allow us to help each other. If only we knew how!

"Confess your faults one to another, and pray one for another, that ye may be healed. The effectual fervent prayer of a righteous man availeth much" (James 5:16).

The need for this knowledge is so desperate, for we lose children to sin when we use wrong methods of correction.

The need is crucial because friendships of a lifetime are broken when one party can no longer take a fault of another and doesn't know how to tell the real reason for running away.

The need should be classified as an emergency since marriages end in divorce simply because the partners do not know how to handle correction of problems in their relationship.

The need is so dramatic because employers often dismiss good employees who could be saved if the boss knew how to correct a problem.

The need is serious! Sunday school children, bus children, and yes, adults, are leaving churches whose teachers lash out instead of using loving correction. "She doesn't know how to correct!" Well, who does?

Let's Start at Home!

Before we try to learn how to give correction, let's start at home by learning how to take correction graciously.

I've always hated to be corrected. I know I need it; it helps me. I have learned to stand still and take it, but something within me wants to rise up and scream bloody murder on the spot when I am corrected. (That's the black dog.)

Now there is a part of me that loves correction and honestly goes toward it. (That's the white dog.) Remember, Christian, there is a new man, a new nature, that, if it is fed properly, can help us lap up correction.

"For which cause we faint not; but though our outward man perish, yet the inward man is renewed day by day" (II Cor. 4:16).

"That ye put off concerning the former conversation the old man, which is corrupt according to the deceitful lusts; And be renewed in the spirit of your mind; And that ye put on the new man, which after God is created in righteousness and true holiness" (Eph. 4:22-24).

Because my black dog has always been fed so well, there is much I do not know and have not accomplished.

I guess almost everyone thinks his mom was the best cook in the world, but it so happens that my mom was, so forget it! I even have facts to prove it. She cooked the meals in our restaurant, and hundreds of people came to buy her food and proclaim it the best.

Now, I should know how to cook all the dishes she could cook. Right? Wrong! Because I would not take correction, I did not learn. Mom wanted to teach me, but she made the "mistake" of telling me what I did wrong. That tended to make me throw up my hands in a nervous frenzy. I also went into hysterics over being corrected at the sewing machine, piano and a few hundred other things; therefore, I remained a stunted dwarf in all those areas. I'm sorry, but we grow in direct proportion to the amount of correction we can take.

I've been known to stay away from people who corrected me. I thought I fixed them! Really, I was fixing myself, in most cases. Oh, I know you sometimes need to stay away from someone who is just nit-picking since that can sap needed confidence. But this is usually not the case.

Have you ever left a church because you were given godly correction from the pulpit? Have you ever seen anyone get up and leave a Sunday school class because she couldn't take correction? This is big stuff I'm talking about. Being able to take correction truly places you in the big leagues!

Here are some verses that teach lessons we should be learning in regard to correction:

Lesson 1: Do not be angry when God corrects you for doing wrong. "My son, despise not the chastening of the Lord; neither be weary of his correction" (Prov. 3:11).

Lesson 2: God corrects only those He loves. "For whom

the Lord loveth he correcteth. . ." (Prov. 3:12).

Lesson 3: A base man hates those who correct him. "Reprove not a scorner, lest he hate thee: rebuke a wise man, and he will love thee" (Prov. 9:8).

Lesson 4: A wise man will love you for correction. "A reproof entereth more into a wise man than an hundred stripes into a fool" (Prov. 17:10).

Lesson 5: Honor is gained by correcting wise men when they are wrong. "He that rebuketh a man afterwards shall find more favour than he that flattereth with the tongue" (Prov. 28:23).

Take It—Right or Wrong!

One time I was the recipient of a truck load of correction. It was as if a dump truck backed up and unloaded on me all at once. This absolutely devastated me for about three weeks. It wasn't handled correctly. Anyone who knew the facts would say so.

A friend (she really was one) had built up resentment about a couple of my attitudes until she could no longer take it. She proceeded to give me a list of about twenty-five things I had done wrong.

My first reaction was to cut her off for life. My second reaction was to tell other friends all about it in order to defend myself and receive sympathy. Way down the list of possible other reactions was the one that said to sift through the debris, pull myself up and see if I could get something out of the load to help me.

It took the white dog three weeks to get up again. The friend and I got together and discovered that all the incidents she gave me filtered down to one attitude I needed to correct.

Each of us learned. She did it all wrong, but I still learned.

It's against all human nature to take correction graciously. I'm sure I'm not the only one who has a natural inclination against it.

"There hath no temptation taken you but such as is common

to man: but God is faithful, who will not suffer you to be tempted above that ye are able; but will with the temptation also make a way to escape, that ye may be able to bear it" (I Cor. 10:13).

You may be the one who explodes on the spot of correction. If so, people will see that they cannot give it to you, and you will be the loser. You will be laid off without being given a reason, or you will be passed over for an opportunity you will never know was available. The fact will be well known. They will say of you, "Don't try to work with so-and-so; she can't take it." You might as well write the letters L-E-P-R-O-S-Y over your head. You're done as far as any real growth is concerned. You'll be limited for life.

If you're asking how you can control yourself at the point of correction—whether given in a right or wrong manner—look for the escape hole. God promised it in I Corinthians 10:13—the verse is given two paragraphs back. It's there if we want it. The escape hole might be planning a stock answer such as, "Let me get away and think about this, and I'll get back to you." In that way you can perform your juvenile antics all by yourself and hope your brain will take over as your glands settle down.

Think Why!

Once your brain (yes, you do have a brain!) begins to function, think about the reason for the correction being given. Why should God allow this to be given? He did allow it (even wrong correction), for He could have killed the person who was giving it, you know.

Begin to examine yourself (no morbid introspection, please).

"Search me, O God, and know my heart: try me, and know my thoughts: And see if there be any wicked way in me, and lead me in the way everlasting" (Ps. 139:23, 24).

"Let the words of my mouth, and the meditation of my heart, be acceptable in thy sight, O Lord, my strength, and my redeemer" (Ps. 19:14).

Thank Him for allowing this in your life; now ask Him to show you why He had to allow it.

"In every thing give thanks: for this is the will of God in Christ Jesus concerning you" (I Thess. 5:18).

"Rejoice in the Lord alway: and again I say, Rejoice" (Phil. 4:4).

Yes, get to the place of thanking Him for something He knows you really need, whether you know it or not. Oh, I know it will take awhile before you can do this. This is a goal; it is not something you will master immediately. You will not automatically begin being able to take a ton of correction off a dump truck while sweetly saying, "Thank you, my dear; please give me more." That's stupid and unrealistic thinking; at least, it sure is for me—wretched sinner that I am.

Be sorry for the person who doesn't know what to do with hostility other than harbor it until she gives a truck load, but be happy for yourself if you can get something from it. That's the goal!

Don't Talk to Others About the Correction!

We are usually our own worst enemies as we spread doubt about ourselves while going to others for sympathy. They may really believe bad things about us after we tell them about all the correction given to us.

Not talking to others is one of the most difficult things to do. After being corrected, the first thing most of us want to do is to go to someone for sympathy. It's natural—from childhood on up. I remember going under the bed with my doll at the age of four. I remember talking to Ginger, the bulldog, at the age of six. I remember climbing into a tree to fume at the branches when my folks failed to understand me, at the age of ten. Then, I remember the really bad things, such as telling other Sunday school classmates about what our Sunday school teacher had done to me.

I wonder if I irreparably hurt some young person as I turned him/her permanently against a teacher by whom I was temporarily hurt. We say, "Good enough for them! People should know what they are like!" We never seem to realize that the one we hurt is not the one on whom we tattled, but the one to whom we told it!

You know how it is. When the preacher questions you about missing church, you tell your sister how gross he was. You get straightened out, go back to church, want her to come with you and find that she now hates the preacher. Keeping our mouths shut during the recovery period following correction is pretty serious business, you see.

Remember how you complained to your friend about your husband? Then you got right with him, only to find your friend gossiping about him, since you have now made her dislike him. You wonder why she feels this way; now you begin having trouble with her.

Beloved, we can't afford to nurse our wounds with others. You ask, "No one?" No one! That is, do not tell unless you want to risk hurting that person's attitude for life. It could happen.

In Christian college work, I've seen some funny things. I once corrected a girl wrongly, who in turn talked against me to her mother. Then her mother had a triple tragedy—and I do mean tragedy—in her life for which it seemed I could have been some help. By then, the girl could not get her mother to come to me because she had caused her to dislike me. The relationship between the girl and me was fine by then, but the wall had been built.

All right, so you see the need for shutting your mouth when hurting after correction. But how do you do it? That's the question! Here are the answers.

Run to God's Word! Right now you're feeling stupid and unloved. Go to the Love Letter for a dose of Scripture on love.

Work! Find some project that involves hard physical labor upon which to "vent your spleen."

While you're working, listen to good music or tapes which will set a mood of healing.

Go toward others! Do something for someone who still has a chance to be someone even if you are so far gone there's no hope. (This feeling will pass—especially as you feel better about yourself while doing for others.)

Have some fun. Take a picnic to a lake. (Make fun for someone else even if you are joyless.) Go visit an old-fashioned town you like.

Do whatever you have to do to keep your mouth shut while your hide is still smarting. Since you see everything out of perspective at this point, you are likely to wound others and thereby heap more hurt on yourself and others if you open your mouth while in this frame of mind.

Reassure Those Who Corrected You!

These are actual letters I have received from girls who are now "on the grow." This takes real Christianity.

> Dear Mrs. Evans:
>
> I thought you would appreciate hearing how one of your tapes helped me in an unusual way.
>
> My youngest daughter is two years old, and some days it seems that if she's not making a mess of one thing, she's breaking something else.
>
> One day recently I was getting really frazzled because of all her antics. I thought, *If that child gets into one more bit of mischief, I'm going to SCREAM!* (Of course, I should have recognized what was happening to me, but I was not wise enough to stop and think.)
>
> A short while later, I walked into the living room to find that she had gotten into my cassette tapes and had one tape all unwound from its cassette. Just as I was about to explode, I read the title on the cassette: "Emotional Control" (Gulp!). Remembering your suggestion on the tape, I took a five-minute "vacation" instead of having the "hissy fit" I had planned to have.
>
> When I came back from my "vacation," I was able to discipline Gretchen in love . . . not punish her in anger. Then, as I slowly rewound the tape by hand, I got really tickled at the

way the Lord had worked in arranging to have that be the tape Gretchen found.

—From Ohio

Mrs. Evans:

I just couldn't escape this opportunity to write you a thank you. You may not remember me, but I spoke to you at the women's conference in 1976.

My life was so discouraging at the time. Thank you so much for correcting and encouraging me. That day you taught a session on purity. Because my parents taught me right, I believed a girl ought to cherish her purity.

The problems that I was facing were my own fault. I was so tired of searching for a young man that had the same convictions. It seemed like there just weren't any. My standards were just too high for them. Before I met you, I had made up my mind to just be an old maid. I had given up as far as a husband was concerned. I mean, I was already 23!

My heart was broken through your ministry. My desire turned to a never-give-up attitude. I was willing to be single all my life, but I didn't feel like I was the single type.

You really encouraged me to keep those standards and wait on the Lord.

The funny part is, after I got a right heart attitude, I met my future husband the next week! Now God has full control. It was His will for me to be a wife. I just had the sin of impatience and trying to plan His timing for things.

—From Virginia

Let me share a letter I received after talking with a "modern" young lady recently.

Dear Mrs. Evans:

I'm sure you are aware of the fact that one of the biggest things I fight is loose or barnyard talk. The conversation with you this morning reminded me so much of my mom because she preached that same thing to me and was appalled at the things I said. But I just always thought she was "old-fashioned" and "behind the times."

Some things really clicked for me as you talked about loose talk: 1. If we do it in private, it will eventually come out in public. 2. Young girls will follow our patterns, and if we talk loosely, they will carry it farther. 3. If I should become a preacher's wife, the women in the church won't respect me if I talk loosely. 4. I realized that it must start with me. I must be careful of the things I say whether in private, in public,

> with close friends or new acquaintances. I must "bury" my barnyard talk.

Why don't you get the syndrome going by sitting down right now and writing Mom and Dad a thank-you letter for loving you enough to correct you? Begin to help your poor befuddled brain to equate love with correction (even if your parents didn't know how to give correction).

Once in a Christian Womanhood class at Hyles-Anderson College, Cindy Hyles Schaap wrote about parents and leaders who had loved her enough to give her correction, after I had asked the class to write out a list of ways their parents showed love to them through correction. Why don't you do this same project and send it to your folks?

Thank people orally. They'll die, but do it anyway! How many times have you had someone tell you that correction you gave them saved them a lot of trouble? Not many, I'm sure. Why don't you be different? Think of someone you can thank, and call them right now. It will begin to put you in the path of correction and therefore growth.

20 – How's Your Balance?

"And Jesus increased in wisdom [mentally] and stature [physically], and in favour with God [spiritually] and man [socially]" (Luke 2:52).

Jesus, the perfect One, gives us an example of balance which we can put before ourselves as a goal to strive toward for a lifetime. If we constantly gain (increase) mentally, physically, spiritually and socially, we'll be pretty well balanced by the time we've worked at it five to ten years.

Please don't gasp at the amount of time mentioned. Remember, most people never approach anything like balance or have any idea of even knowing to want it. Also, you might want to recall that circus performers spend grueling hours daily learning to perform balancing acts.

Another thing to be aware of is that once the balancing act is learned, much practice is required in order to maintain that learning!

Balance is evidently important, for thousands of people spend hundreds of dollars to watch elephants balance on little stools, monkeys balance on bicycles, seals balance balls on their noses, and fifty other balancing acts.

I am told that balance has a great deal to do with all sports. There is also the balance of nature to take into account. Artists and musicians talk about balance. Even a washing machine will quit when it gets out of balance! Our big toes have a lot to do with our balance and are so vital. Inner ear trouble causes havoc because it affects the balance. Indeed, balance is worth acquiring.

Do We Really Lack Balance?

We would have to say that many of us really do lack balance. A boy looking for a date has a difficult time choosing between a fun girl or a lady-like girl. He sometimes finds that he has to choose between a girl who has time to do anything anytime but is lazy, and one who is too busy to ever do anything spontaneously.

Many a husband has had to choose between a housekeeper and a party girl, or between a spendthrift and a wife who can balance a checkbook but cannot enjoy much fun.

In 1979 I wrote the following while sitting in Sunday school listening to Brother Hyles, and after he said something that caused my heart to respond in earnest pleas:

O LORD, HELP ME TO BE:
Firm but not harsh;
Realistic but not skeptical;
Scheduled but not rigid;
Pure but not proud;
Close-mouthed but not unfriendly;
Appropriate but not stiff;
Funny but not frivolous;
Teachable but not gullible;
Flexible but not scatterbrained;
Humble but not pious;
Kind but not compromising;
Dependable but not dull;
Decisive but not stubborn;
Persistent but not needling;
Precise but not picky;
Simple but not foolish;
Demanding but not intolerant;
Thorough but not unkind;
Human but not worldly;

Spiritual but not impractical;
Generous but not irresponsible;
Enthusiastic but not "hyper";
Honest but not brutal;
Fair but not unloving;
Proper but not unreal;
Confident but not snobbish;
Bold but not brazen;
Busy but not harried;
Active but not shallow;
Deep but not dry;
Wise but not intimidating;
Intense but not forbidding;
Empathetic but not uncontrolled;
Forgiving but not naive;
Sympathetic but not pitying;
Helpful but not condescending;
Penitent but not paralyzed;
Organized but not bossy;
Spontaneous but not inconsistent.

Lord, I guess I'm asking that You help me grow in favor with God and man. I am asking Your help in becoming a balanced person. Amen.

After reading my imploring words, do you relate to my feelings of a lack of balance? Then you, too, understand the following: "I feel like I've got a three-ring circus going. I get one ring going well, and the others fall apart. I begin the ring of church work, and the house goes to pot! I get the housework going well, and the Sunday school class and my kids are neglected."

These are sad words I've just given you—so sad that they often spell failure, disgrace and humiliation.

How many times have we seen not only individuals but whole households or Christian organizations go under because of a lack of balance!

I once knew a fine leader in a Christian work who began to be mightily used of God. People poured in to hear him preach and to get his help. No one, including himself, said he knew anything about business. He was able to help people, that's all!

That ability seemingly ruined him. He found himself running a huge organization made necessary in order to handle the crowds who came for help. Pressure in an area about which he knew little led to shortcuts and finally disaster. There were those who called him a crook. A good man apparently was lost to Christian work because of a lack of balance. If only he could have had somewhere to go for help.

If you've never understood the supposed "crooks" as outlined above, perhaps you more fully understand the person who carefully budgets every item down to the last penny. People say, "You don't have to worry about this person, because your money is watched more closely than that of the U.S. Mint." (Sorry for the poor parallel!) But so many times the person who watches the money so closely is so busy "watchdogging" that he never has time to speak to anyone, and he makes those who are not watchdogs feel put down.

May I interrupt here to talk about a balanced lady? She is Mrs. Earlyne Stephens, bursar of Hyles-Anderson College, who watches our money in such a way that we can pay our bills. She also loves us, encourages us and smiles while she's watching it.

How many ladies could write, speak with enthusiasm and also balance the books, all for the Lord and His work? Mrs. Stephens does!

How Do You Get Fixed?

You say, "Okay, Marlene, I'm convinced I need balance; I want to get fixed. I want someone to be able to use me as a balanced lady."

I'll give you an example of the "talk out of both sides of our mouths" that will begin to get us fixed. Yes, we just need to be fixed.

This balance, or lack of it, came into focus in a big way the other day when two who work in my office were confronted with the month's telephone bill. The person responsible for paying the bill was overwhelmed by the amount. (Are you relating to this?) Because she was so distressed, she began interrogation:

"Who made this call?" "Whom were you calling?" "How long did you talk?" "Was it really business?"

I guess I should be glad she was just interrogating instead of making wild implications of thievery, as I have heard some checkers of telephone bills do.

The person being interrogated wrote me a big note:

> If I'm going to be accused of stealing, I will have to work someplace else. I was just doing my work—what I was supposed to be doing, I thought. Here is money for the old stupid telephone bill! I will be glad to pay it personally if she thinks I'm cheating!

Here's where "talking out of both sides of your mouth" helps a whole lot. I definitely believe in it. I do it so much that each person thinks I'm for the other one and not for her! Oops! Am I unbalanced in that, too?!

I do want them to know I'm for taking the other person's part for the good of the person to whom I am speaking. If I can help the one I'm dealing with to understand another, I'll truly be for her.

I said to the payer of the telephone bill:

> Yes, she does talk longer than you would. She also thinks some calls are business calls that you would not consider business calls. Why is that, do you suppose? What does our organization get from her "wheeler-dealer" freedom with the telephone? How can we help her to continue giving us the strength and yet help her with this seeming weakness?

Of course, I'm shortening the conversation and not giving you all the words when I gave my plea for the offender. I did ask that she empathize the next time before slapping down a bill in front of a person and demanding, "What's this? The telephone is going to have to be taken out because we can't pay our bill." I also told her she might not be able to feel with the telephone offender since she was the type who might use a three-minute egg-timer for the one long-distance call she would make in a decade. Then I told her she could feel with the offender if she would stop and think of her attitude toward people. Some think she is a "wheeler-dealer" in throwing around directions when not asked. She doesn't even know she's doing it. Neither does the telephone offender know she's talking all those hours. (You know how it is. Remember the time your child said, "Mommy, Mommy, I want you," to which you replied, "I'll be off the phone in a minute"? Did you ever time that minute? Did you ever time yourself between that point and the point when the child picks up a peanut butter jar and drops it?)

Next, I had the telephone offender on my hands. She was hurt, crushed, humiliated and defensive (to name only a few adjectives that described her feelings following the confrontation). I had to spend the first portion of our time together just trying to convince her that I didn't think she was a thief, a crook nor a cheat and that the payer of bills didn't think so either. Then I said something like this:

> Aren't we glad we have someone who cares about the bills? That is why we get our paychecks on time every month. It must be difficult for her to know how to check the phone bill in a way which does not seem offensive and accusative. Can you imagine what an unpopular position that would be if you were in it? She probably feels completely devastated when she gets those bills and does not know where she'll get the money to pay all of them. I wouldn't want her job, would you? What do you think we could do to help her?

As long as we're unbalanced and imperfect, we'll have to endure things such as this or go through life completely bewildered and puzzled about Christians and their "harsh, accusing ways," or Christians and their "lying, stealing and/or cheating."

Now if your church, home and organization were full of Mrs. Stephenses, you would be okay and wouldn't need to talk out of "both sides of your mouth." Oh, by the way, call me collect to tell me if you do have a church, home or organization full of balanced people. I will apply for a position there immediately. But then, I'd put it out of balance; so on second thought, forget it!

Since you can detect my skepticism, I might as well confess that I truly believe I will need to learn to champion unbalanced people for the rest of my life. In light of that fact, I once wrote down these thoughts:

Be Ye Kind

"And be ye kind one to another, tenderhearted, forgiving one another, even as God for Christ's sake hath forgiven you" (Eph. 4:32).

Let's ask God to help us accept HIS acceptance of us so that we can accept all others before we know all the unacceptable about them!

1. I don't like the way she acts—as if she thinks she's "It," but I can forget that, as I love her for the way she takes care of big projects that need to be tackled.
2. I don't like the way she keeps bugging me every time I happen to see her, but I can forget that, as I love her for the way she tries to learn.
3. I don't like the way she's so scatterbrained, but I can forget that, as I love her for the fun she brings into a room with her.
4. I don't like her dullness, but I can forget that, as I love her for being the one who sees that the tiny details are cared for as we prepare for an activity.
5. I don't like her slow actions, but I can forget that, as I love her for her gentle way with children.
6. I don't like the way she puts herself down all the time, but I can forget that, as I love her for her desire to please others.
7. I don't like the way she talks incessantly, but I can forget that, as I love her for the interest she shows in times of need.
8. I don't like the way she makes me feel put down when I'm around her, but I can forget that, as I love her for her example in dress.
9. I don't like the way she stands around waiting for someone else to make every move, but I can forget that, as I love her for the way she accepts leadership.

10. I don't like her bossy, takeover methods, but I can forget that, as I love her for helping me to do good things I would never have done without her.

11. I don't like her harsh words and blunt ways, but I can forget that, as I love her for her sincere determination.

12. I don't like her kindness to my face as she slyly gets her point over to me, but I can forget that, as I love her for the effort she feels she's making to protect my feelings.

13. I don't like her inattention to detail, but I can forget that, as I love her for the friendliness she shows to all people.

14. I don't like her poor grooming, but I can forget that, as I love her for "digging in" to accomplish any old task.

15. I don't like her filthy room, but I can forget that, as I love her for her ability to drop everything to help me.

Yes, as long as we live in an unbalanced world of unbalanced people, we will have to accept each other for what we are if we are ever to have a ghost of a chance to help with what we are not!!

Just maybe, only perhaps, but just possibly, we will grow more balanced and "get fixed" as we champion every person and see the good side, the balance, in each one. That way we'll be mostly looking to good, for we'll block the bad. This will expose us to balance.

As always, God was planning for our good when He drew up the blueprints for love, compassion and mercy! If we forgive others, we are able to love them for what they are. Therefore, we'll be in constant contact with the good of every person. This has to work for our eventual balance. Wow! What a thought!

How Can I Learn to Look at the Good?

Again, my natural cynicism is going to show, but if you are as depraved as I, you'll have to start from the bad and work toward the good. I wish it weren't so, but it is with most of us.

Those of you who think good thoughts naturally won't have

need of this; but wait! Please read on anyway just so you'll understand the rest of us. It will give you balance in understanding people.

Please don't wring your hands as you say, "I can't learn this. I've always had stinkin' thinkin'; I've been taught that kind of thinking, and I will always have it." Again, there's a balance between blaming yourself for everything (which is a way of excusing ourselves from taking any future positive action) and blaming everyone and everything else for that which happens to you.

We will have to practice this as we used to practice our A, B, C's and 1, 2, 3's. For a moment sit quietly and remember the difficulty you had with the A, B, C's in first grade. I can remember what seat I was in and the hopeless feeling I had in the East Ward School when Miss Craig pointed to new letters (with a long, wooden, hooked pointer) when I hadn't yet learned the old ones. We'd better go slower than Miss Craig went.

Let's Do Some A, B, C Thinking!

"A" stands for "awful thinking." "B" stands for "bad thinking." "C" stands for "caring thinking."

Now, proceed with caution as you practice thinking.

Let's try some A, B, C's that you might need. Maybe one of these examples should be your thinking.

A: "I don't like that woman. Her clothes are so worldly. Look at that tight dress; it shows every move of her fat body."

B: "I need to tell her that she looks as bad as a woman of the street."

C: "That woman probably didn't have a mother like mine who lovingly taught me how to dress and why I should dress right. She surely is a lot of fun though. Her husband seems happy. I wonder if she'd help me learn to be fun."

Result: As I give vibrations that show I approve of her fun, she can afford to learn from me how to dress. This is called getting and giving balance. "And Jesus increased in wisdom and stature, and in favour with God and man" (Luke 2:52).

A: "That woman grates on my nerves something terrible. I can't stand to be around her. She's a loud, bossy cow."

B: "I wish someone would put that woman in her place" (and what we mean by "her place" cannot be written in a Christian publication).

C: "God has blessed me with a soft-voiced mother who helped me to learn graciousness at her knee. That woman seems as if she'd like to be able to help us organize our visitation program. She probably could help me go out to visit."

Result: As I learn how to go toward people, she learns how to keep the people she knows how to go toward; it is called balance.

A: "That woman has a stinkin' house. How can she teach a Sunday school class? If I were she, I'd be ashamed to stand before young girls."

B: "Someone ought to tell that woman to stay home and get her own house clean before she tries to clean up Sunday school girls' lives."

C: "Mom always kept a clean house, with everything in its place. I don't even remember her having to teach it to me. I just picked it up from her. However, I surely don't remember picking up the speaking ability that woman seems to have when she talks to her Sunday school class."

Result: As I ask that woman for teaching tips, she can afford to say, "My house really bothers me." That gives me the opportunity to work with her on what my mother taught me.

No, we don't learn to look at the good easily. It comes hard, like the A, B, C's and the 1, 2, 3's. It is long division, multiplication and everything else rolled up into one.

Before you wring your hands over the dirty house of another woman, saying, "How can I tell her?" look to see what you can learn from her. Then she'll probably let you help her. Remember:

when you want to help someone else, go in all honesty to ask for help from her.

It's my dream—my goal—my desire—my wish—my prayer—that I will someday be the person who will accept unbalanced people to the point that they can learn from me and that they'll accept me to the point that I can afford to learn from them!

Again, if a person has a dirty house, don't tell her; don't ask to clean it for her, but do start learning something from her!

It's my dream that there will be more balanced ladies someday. Until then, let's accept each other for what we are. Right now, we're going to have to accept a good Sunday school teacher along with her dirty house.

We need the fun of the poorly dressed woman. May she have sense of humor enough to remain teachable and to learn to dress properly.

Let's accept a strength of a person, use that strength and enjoy it; but remember: we will also have to accept the corresponding weakness unless balance has taken place.

When was the last time your washer went out of balance? Mine knocked around so much it began climbing the stairs! (Only kidding!) First of all, it got out of balance because I distributed the clothes wrongly. Many times people are out of balance partly because of wrong handling by us. Second, we don't usually throw the washer or kick it when it gets out of balance. If we do, we're temporarily insane with anger and frustration. We are also temporarily insane if we kick or throw out an out-of-balance person. We fix or get the washer fixed, and sometimes it seems to take forever.

Enough said? Let's go fix and be fixed. You, then, will be balanced for beauty!

21 – A Dirty Bible

My Bible is clean and neat—way too clean and neat for the type person I am. Now, I realize that there are those of you who can get the Word of God into you without destroying the printed page; however, I also know there are others of you who are relating to me.

Those books which you most enjoy are marked (with pencil, red pen, blue pen, black pen and crayon) and spattered with food and/or drink. They may even wear grease, makeup, sand or dirt. You take them wherever you go, bend their backs, toss them around and do all kinds of despicable things to them. This is not good. Any librarian or teacher will tell you this is bad, bad, bad! I've believed them to the point that I've hurt my life. I've taken care of my Bible at the expense of caring for my heart!

Make a Decision!

I received a new Bible which was small enough to carry in a big purse and just large enough to contain the type of print I can read with my bifocals. It was presented to me on the 26th day of August, 1980, on the occasion of my decision to have a dirty Bible.

I'm happy to say that the lines under the verses are crooked. That means I didn't wait for ideal circumstances in order to study my Bible. I just hauled it out of my purse while sitting in the K-Mart parking lot waiting for our son to gather his school supplies on his own. There was no ruler or heavy 3″x5″ card handy; so I marked any ol' way I wanted and had thirty to forty minutes of fun in the verses which jumped out at me that day.

I had been ashamed of my clean Bible. It told a story I was not proud to admit. I was not made for new clothes. Shoes that stick around me show wear in only a few days. Connie Brown says certain types of furniture just don't go with my lifestyle. I use, and I'm afraid sometimes abuse, things! I'm one of those people about whom they say, "Her house looks lived in." That's a nice way of saying, "It's not clean, but there's a path shoveled through."

I've often tried to change this. I still hope I can learn to take better care of things. However, at this point I'm at the stage in life of, "Clothes, stay with me. We're going through!" It's terrible to catch your pocket on a doorknob and be halfway down the block before finding out your jacket won't reach!

Now, if you are hopelessly like me or know anyone in such a state, don't give up or encourage others to give up the fight to be better. But don't wait until you get all better to get into your Bible. It's better to have a messed-up Bible than a messed-up life.

Take your Bible on the walk along the beach. Indiana Dunes State Park is about forty-five minutes from us. I've enjoyed the cranes, the waves, the soft clean sand, the sunset, the rain, the rocks, the trees—and the Bible. Sometimes it gets mixed up with potato chips and tuna sandwiches; but grease spots of tuna now mean something special to me. Those smears mean that my Bible is a part of my life.

Run to the Bible!

If I'm going to live anywhere close to a victorious Christian life, I'll have to run to the Bible—not walk, not tiptoe, not crawl, but run to the Bible! That means I must have a copy of the Word of God always handy. I never know when I'm going to need it desperately. I'm not talking about the regular devotion time or the Sunday school lesson study time, but about the times when we run into "brick walls" every way we turn. I'm talking about the times people seem to delight in "getting us." In other words, I'm describing hours of frustration, hurt, guilt and self-pity.

Then, there are those real heart-stoppers and heartbreakers—the times when we lose jobs, health, mate or children. At those times we often wonder how anyone goes through it without the Lord. Yet, we're not even in the Bible habit enough to know how to apply what the Lord has given us for such times.

Get the Bible Habit!

People who are addicted to cigarettes carry a pack within reach at all times. They place them by their bedsides so they can smoke just before going to bed and immediately upon awaking. Some folks even wake up during the night to be soothed back to sleep by a cigarette. If a real tobacco addict is caught without his cigarettes, an emergency is declared while new supplies are found.

I really hate to make a parallel between something so harmful as nicotine and something so helpful as the Bible, but I wish we would go after the Bible with a bit of the same fervor as a smoker goes after his cigarettes.

"Foodaholics" begin to shake after a couple of hours without refueling. Weight Watchers recognizes this phenomenon and works around the principle of piling loads of food (the right kinds) into the body at scheduled intervals. Weight-Watcher people travel with fruit, vegetables and other approved goodies so as not to be caught someplace without food.

As people have to have food, tobacco, drugs and alcohol, I want to have to have the Word of God. I want to have to have the Bible regularly. I want to have to have the Bible when I'm knocked down. I want to have to have the Bible when I go to bed. I want to have to have the Bible when I get up in the morning. And I want to have to have the Bible when I wake up in the night. That means, at this point in my life, I'll have a dirty Bible.

One day, chipper as I could be, I walked into the hall leading to my office at the college. I was going in to work on a special project which I had planned all day. I felt good. Then, a girl met me with a few words that just devastated me! It wasn't all that bad, but the words recalled to mind a whole series of similar negative incidents.

I ran to my office, grabbed my Bible, quickly opened it to Psalms, hugged it to my heart, and then began reading at random. I was so out of perspective that I couldn't really think where to look for help. I just let the words of the Psalms calm me and put me back into working order.

Those words kept me from bawlin' and squallin'; they kept me from running to cause trouble for and with people as I told them my "tragedy." I was soon on my way to the beginning of healing and could even function at the project I had planned. I didn't have to go home to bed with a "sick" headache—whatever that is. Instead, I read Psalm 40:1-5:

"I waited patiently for the Lord; and he inclined unto me, and heard my cry. He brought me up also out of an horrible pit, out of the miry clay, and set my feet upon a rock, and established my goings. And he hath put a new song in my mouth, even praise unto our God: many shall see it, and fear, and shall trust in the Lord. Blessed is that man that maketh the Lord his trust, and respecteth not the proud, nor such as turn aside to lies. Many, O Lord my God, are thy wonderful works which thou hast done, and thy thoughts which are to us-ward: they cannot be reckoned up in order unto thee: if I would declare and speak of them, they are more than can be numbered."

I also read Psalm 37:1-10:

"Fret not thyself because of evildoers, neither be thou envious against the workers of iniquity. For they shall soon be cut down like the grass, and wither as the green herb. Trust in the Lord, and do good; so shalt thou dwell in the land, and verily thou shalt be fed. Delight thyself also in the Lord; and he shall give thee the desires of thine heart. Commit thy way unto the Lord; trust also in him; and he shall bring it to pass. And he shall bring forth thy righteousness as the light, and thy judgment as the noonday. Rest in the Lord, and wait patiently for him: fret not thyself because of him who prospereth in his way, because of the man who bringeth wicked devices to pass. Cease from anger, and forsake wrath: fret not thyself in any wise to do evil. For evildoers shall be cut off: but those that wait upon the Lord, they shall inherit the earth. For yet a little while, and the wicked shall not be: yea, thou shalt diligently consider his place, and it shall not be."

These Scriptures and portions of a dozen other Psalms don't go side by side with foolish behavior in the wake of a storm of life.

Keep Some With You

Our feelings are so fickle that we can be doing pretty well after we run for a dose of Scripture; then, we can be attacked again as we go on with our work. If you're hurting before you go to bed, grab a phrase to keep on your mind when you turn out the lights. You might be clobbered (mentally) in the dark. Perhaps you read Philippians 4:4-9. Something like ". . . and the God of peace shall be with you" will steady you. Roll it over and over in your mind, and let it put you into a peaceful sleep.

You know how you do with bottles of perfume or hand lotion. You keep a small purse-size container with you whenever possible. I want to have to have small portions of the Bible with me at all times.

Don't Flirt With the Bible!

A friend of mine went to my husband for counsel, asking, "How can I live the Christian life as I should?" She told me that my husband threw the Bible on the desk and said, "That's the answer."

The friend said, "I'm not reading the Bible like I used to. It seems as if I've gotten so busy that now I just do my duty-reading."

My husband told her how she could get her enjoyment back immediately. He suggested she take her Bible and go to the woods two days in a row, with no other book and no people.

She and I figured she must be having only a flirtation with the Bible. She wasn't getting the comfort, guidance, security or discipline that she had been getting when she was having a love relationship with the Word of God. It's sort of like a child being swatted at but not really spanked; this leaves only a feeling of frustration. We need to let the Bible spank us and then let it love us.

Let's Have a Sweet Love Relationship With the Bible!

A love relationship with the Bible will meet all your needs. It will cause you to find the way to be approved by God: "Study to shew thyself approved unto God, a workman that needeth not to be ashamed, rightly dividing the word of truth" (II Tim. 2:15).

It will help you grow in the Lord: "As newborn babes, desire the sincere milk of the word, that ye may grow thereby" (I Pet. 2:2).

Look what else it will do for you:

"And that from a child thou hast known the holy scriptures, which are able to make thee wise unto salvation through faith which is in Christ Jesus. All scripture is given by inspiration of God, and is profitable for doctrine, for reproof, for correction, for instruction in righteousness: That the man of God may be perfect, throughly furnished unto all good works" (II Tim. 3:15-17).

There's no substitute for victory, and victory comes through the Word of God! If the things you love really show use, set a goal with me—that of having a dirty Bible.

"For the word of God is quick, and powerful, and sharper than any twoedged sword, piercing even to the dividing asunder of soul and spirit, and of the joints and marrow, and is a discerner of the thoughts and intents of the heart" (Heb. 4:12).

22 – Becoming a Classic

One day I told our son David why I liked his name. To me it seems to be one of those names that never go out of style.

The name "David" has been "in" since Bible times for sure. When you see the name, you can't associate it with one era only. It isn't trendy. It's a classic.

When Connie Brown talks and writes about Christians looking nice without spending an exorbitant amount of money, she invariably brings up the issue of buying classics—those good quality garments which have had a charm for one hundred years or more. A girl at school came back after Christmas wearing a gray wool pleated skirt her aunt had worn in high school thirty years ago. I thought it was brand new! I believe that is what Connie Brown means when she discusses classics in clothes.

John R. Rice Classics

One of the Hyles-Anderson College Bible teachers published an article in *Christian Womanhood* which stated:

> I honestly believe that few men will, in a whole lifetime of ministry, match the contribution Dr. John R. Rice has made in writing any of these three books. To produce one classic is a rare achievement; to write three is a miracle; to write them on the side, while staying busy as editor and evangelist, is staggering! (The three books referred to are: *Prayer: Asking and Receiving, Our God-Breathed Book—the Bible* and *The Power*

> *of Pentecost.)* These are the best books in print in their fields, and (barring the rapture) will last for centuries.

I have found there are lasting pieces of furniture and china. Connie Brown has the same fine taste with home furnishings that she has in clothing selection. She has helped me look for good pieces of furniture I could buy as inexpensively as possible. A year or so ago she called to say she had found a used, round, walnut, gateleg table. She felt it would suit the needs of my small dining room. Because I don't have an eye for that kind of thing, I would never have noticed the table had I been browsing through the junk shop—pardon me, the antique shop! When I went to look at it, I found the price to be right, so I said, "If Connie says it's okay, I want it. I've seen her home. I trust her taste."

Well, that little old gateleg table has really grown on me! Know what I mean? There are things that get better the longer you're with them. The table has a little drawer from which a seasonal decoration peeks at us as we leave it pulled out a bit. One time Pat Hays was leafing through a new Ethan Allen catalog and found a picture of that very table. That old $185 table can be purchased new at great expense. I have a classic. Its worth will not diminish by use or time!

When I sold china for a few years, I earned many place settings as contest awards. At that time, a plain white pattern with a silver rim around the edge was the rage for girls in their teens and twenties.

Mrs. T. G. Green, a lady who entertained a great deal and one who had collected several sets of china during her years of marriage, was my sales manager. She told me that "Old Rose" was the more lasting pattern—the one girls would treasure more as they became middle-aged and older.

That didn't make much sense to me then, but it does now. Oh, well—if you can have several sets of china, you can afford to have a "fun pattern." You can even have one just suited for sunny breakfasts or Christmas holidays. But if you can have only one pattern, then think what you will like for a lifetime. Don't be tricked by a fad.

My favorite song at one time was, "The Wise Man Built His House Upon a Rock." At another time in my life a favorite was, "Teenager, Are You Lonely?" I still like these choruses. There's nothing wrong with them. When I was a kid, I listened to the old Blackwood Brothers Quartet on a Shenandoah, Iowa station. I just got so excited when they came on the air with their theme song, "Give the World a Smile Each Day." I still like to hear it for my own entertainment.

I went to Bob Jones University and heard Dr. Bob Jones, Sr., say, "Learn the classic hymns of the Faith, the ones which have stood the test of time. Major on the music that tells what God has done through the ages, rather than on your feelings for a moment."

I didn't exactly understand then, but now I find myself being drawn to "The Old Rugged Cross" and "What a Friend We Have in Jesus." I hate to admit it, but I relate to the same hymns the older people ask for over and over in the rest homes.

There's classic beauty. I used to look at Jessie Rice Sandberg and think that she had old-fashioned beauty. That in itself was not a put-down in any way. I did not think she looked old-fashioned in the negative sense of the meaning. However, I later discovered I didn't even mean that she had just old-fashioned beauty. To my way of thinking, she has classic beauty. She'll never go out of style.

Classic or *classical* are words teamed up with descriptions such as: "first class, highest rank, approved, lasting value, standard, authoritative and balanced."

Classic does not mean just "old." That is not enough. Many things that are old were fads in their time and have not been used since their time. Classic does not have "a time"; it's ageless and "era-less."

Businesses That Are Classical

I like businesses which tell me what they are by their names. When I think of Sears, Roebuck and Company, I think of long years of practice of a motto, "Satisfaction guaranteed or your money back." In years past, I have tested that policy often and find that the company stands by its word. Sears has become a classic in business since it never varies from its word.

Mayo Clinic still follows the decision of the father of Will and Charles Mayo, the old country doctor who never withheld help because of financial inability to pay. At Mayo Clinic no mention of money is made until a patient checks out at the end of his stay. If the patient can pay or give proof of insurance, he does; if he can't he's asked to pay as he can.

Mayo is a rare and classic name in the field of medicine; not just because of its modern buildings and equipment, but because of the policies of an old country doctor who operated on people while they were lying on kitchen tables.

Other names that come to mind are as varied as Blue Cross and Blue Shield, A&W Root Beer, Fanny Mae Candy, Campbell's Soup, Heinz Catsup, Oldsmobile, Van Camp Pork and Beans, Skippy Peanut Butter, Butte Knit suits and Butternut coffee. Frigidaire was such a respected brand that many people call all refrigerators Frigidaires!

Some of the respected names in business will not join the ranks of the classics. Though they've lasted a good many years, they are being swayed by the times.

Walt Disney Enterprises have produced classic cartoons; Mickey Mouse is now over fifty years old and shows no signs of losing ground. The "big guys" are toying with the idea of going relevant! They feel they've done all they can to "last through" the years of the "New Morality." If they yield, they will not go down as a classic in their field! If they don't yield, they will come back in style!

Holiday Inn motels were begun in 1955 by men who wanted

there to be "no surprise" when they checked in with family or business friends. They founded their organization on a check list of those things that could be counted on if the sign read, "Holiday Inn."

That dependability was so appreciated that the business boomed to a point beyond supervision. Many Inns follow the check list, but some do not. It looks doubtful as to its becoming a classic business.

In this day and age of changing values and lack of family ties, classics are even more rare.

Above All Else, Be Classical

I recently read a newspaper article in which *classical* was defined, "That which passes the test of time undiminished."

The following words were written by Harold Balke Walker in the *Chicago Tribune* on January 11, 1981:

> In many ways our society has witnessed a decline of the classical, filled as it has been with the trivialities of television. We have saturated ourselves with transient satisfactions that leave us poorer, not richer.
>
> In some areas we have done better, having created such things as computers and ships to explore space and probe Saturn with its rings and moons. These achievements will bear the passing of time undiminished and bear fruit for generations to come.
>
> As for the material aspects of our lives, we are obviously more comfortable than our ancestors. Comfort, however, does not necessarily lead us to standards of value that do not diminish with the passing of time.
>
> Capacity to discard the trivial and the worthless and to cling to the classical is the priceless ingredient in a life that in the end passes the test of time undiminished.

The rules of honesty and good faith, truth and integrity, love and compassion provide a foundation for lives that can be termed classical. Belief in the necessity for obedience to the laws of God leads to a quality of life that is able to pass the test of time undiminished.

We Need Classics!

I believe we need a Mrs. John R. Rice, a Mrs. Bob Jones, Sr., a Mrs. Lee Roberson and a Mrs. Jack Hyles. I don't think we need the old-fashioned. I don't think we need the relevant up-to-dater. We need the one who is for all times!

Do you want to be a classic? Then go to the One who is "the same yesterday, and to day and for ever" (Heb. 13:8) for "classic lessons." He will teach you to be of value for time and eternity. You'll never have to be a "has been" with Jesus as your Teacher. We have classics in books, songs, people, furniture, clothes, china, businesses and even cartoons; but the ultimate, the greatest example of a classic is our Teacher who is our Saviour, Jesus Christ. He is so far beyond any other example of that which does not diminish with time that it seems frivolous to even mention Him in the same sentence with the rarest of any other type classic.

"In the beginning was the Word, and the Word was with God, and the Word was God. The same was in the beginning with God. All things were made by him; and without him was not any thing made that was made. In him was life; and the life was the light of men. And the light shineth in darkness; and the darkness comprehended it not. There was a man sent from God, whose name was John. The same came for a witness, to bear witness of that Light, that all men through him might believe. He was not that Light, but was sent to bear witness of that Light. That was the true Light, which lighteth every man that cometh into the world. He was in the world, and the world was made by him, and the world knew him not. He came unto his own, and his own received him not. But as many as received him, to them gave he power to become the sons of God, even to them that believe on his name: Which were born, not of blood, nor of the will of the flesh, nor of the will of man, but of God. And the Word was made flesh, and dwelt among us, (and we beheld his glory, the glory as of the only begotten of the Father,) full of grace and truth" (John 1:1-14).

"I am Alpha and Omega, the beginning and the end, the first and the last" (Rev. 22:13).

Yes, there's a Book and a Teacher for "classic lessons." Let's begin!

23 — Flip-Side Thinking!

Let's turn to the flip-side!

Most of you no longer have your music on records; it is now on cassettes. But I can remember that when we did have records we would often say, "Turn it to the flip-side."

Christians should not have "bad days," because there's always the flip-side. Now I am not one of those motivational speakers who believes that you can just quote twenty-five times, "I can do all things through Christ," when you don't even know Him as your Saviour, and live a victorious life because you chanted the verse. You must have Jesus Christ. You must have a time when you know you accepted Him as your personal Saviour.

When I talk about the flip-side, I am talking about born-again Christians who, with the power of Christ in them, can go about their daily duties being joyful, victorious, happy, fulfilled, contented and blessed because they know Jesus as their Saviour. They can do this in the midst of a death in the family, in the midst of financial disaster, in the midst of a traffic jam or in the midst of missing the bus to work!

Unfortunately, we Christians do not act much different from the world (meaning someone who doesn't know Christ as his personal Saviour). The world curses when someone pulls in front of them in traffic. Perhaps we Christians don't actually curse, but we give ugly looks, mutter under our breath and let it ruin our day. And we have probably cut in front of someone else one time or many times.

If someone hurts our feelings, we are down for the day. Many of us say, "I haven't had a good day." My goodness! Christians, we who know we are going to Heaven, should never have a bad day! There might be a day when we are in pain, but He is with us. He will not forsake us; He will not leave us; He will comfort us; He will be right by us.

There might be a day when we are struggling for our last breath and waiting to go on to be with Jesus, but how can going to be with Jesus make it a bad day? There is no "bad day" for a Christian.

You're wrong to say, "I've had a really bad morning." You have only had a morning with some problems. That's only realistic. Of course you will have problems at some point in time; but we Christians have the Holy Spirit to help us work through those problems step by step and get our minds on the good things as we work through them. Not one Christian should ever say she has had a bad week, a bad day, a bad morning, a bad hour, a bad minute. There is no bad time for the Christian! We have the Holy Spirit in us, we have Jesus Christ to talk to, and He bids us come to Him and He will give us rest. We have God the Father to go to when dying. So we have no bad times. Just turn your record: flip-side thinking is the answer!

Some of us are on the negative side of the record—the rock and roll side, the bad side, the ugly side. Let's flip that record. The minute you start saying bad about someone, say to yourself, *Flip it!* That might sound a bit slangy, but I don't mean it that way. Just say something that will remind you that your thinking is bad. If we do our thinking on the flip-side, we won't dwell on the negatives. We won't say things or do things we shouldn't (which could really cause us to feel bad all day because we caused everyone around us to feel bad).

Now stop and think a minute. Isn't there a bad and good side to absolutely everything in life—every situation, person and place?

What about your house? Maybe it's big and beautiful. But then, you have to pay higher insurance and more upkeep and maintenance for a larger house. If you lost it, you would just flip your thinking and think about the cons of the big house—the liabilities. But while you have it, dwell on the pros or assets. Think how wonderful it is that God gave you a big house to use for entertaining for His glory. You can keep missionaries or evangelists who need a place to stay. But if you lose it, think, *Boy, I'll enjoy a smaller house! It will be easier to take care of. And the insurance and taxes will be much cheaper.*

Perhaps you have some recreational vehicles—a dirt bike or a boat or an antique car. You have been fortunate (by the world's standards) to have fun things with which to play.

But then all of a sudden you don't have them anymore. When you have them, you should be thankful. You can use them to relax with your family. But when they are gone, then think of the money you are saving by not having them!

So be flexible, be dynamic! A dynamic person is a growing person. He/she isn't particularly one who talks fast and loud and has a very bubbly, outgoing personality. A dynamic person can be quiet and calm. But a dynamic person can go with whatever happens. I am sorry to say that some lost people seem to be able to do that better than some Christians.

Someone asked me the other day, "How can a woman change out of her bad ways of thinking as she matures and gets older?" I believe women pretty much go out of this life like they were when they were younger. If you practice this flip-side thinking when you are young, you will probably go out of life a sweet, elderly lady. But if you always see the bad side, you will go out a bitter, mean old woman.

I don't like the term, "old woman." But when a woman is

mean, people will usually call her the "old woman" in a mean, disparaging way, no matter if she is forty or seventy. There is nothing wrong with being old. But if a woman is sweet, she won't usually be called the "old woman" in a negative way.

But let's say you are already up in years and you stay on the negative side of the record. You can still practice and try to change. It will be more difficult—just like memorizing Scripture is harder when you are older—but it can be done. It just depends on how much you want to change. You can stop yourself when you start being negative and say, *Flip it!* Claim Matthew 5:6 which says, "Blessed are they which do hunger and thirst after righteousness: for they shall be filled."

I would venture to say that all of our unhappiness is because we do not learn to dwell in the land of the good side. It seems that the bad pulls our attention so much more quickly than the good. But then, is it any wonder? Because being sinners, we don't seek after God naturally. Romans 3:10 and 11: "As it is written, There is none righteous, no, not one: There is none that understandeth, there is none that seeketh after God." So, of course, that bad will take our attention so much faster.

You are probably thinking, *If I have no good in me, how will I learn to look at the good side of things?* Perhaps you think you cannot win this battle because you were brought up in a negative atmosphere; perhaps you were taught to dwell in the land of the bad.

Well, almost all of us have been brought up in the land of the bad as far as negative thinking is concerned. In fact, it is just considered the great American pastime. The going philosophy says, "If you think bad, go ahead and say it. Go ahead and think anything you want to." And we are told not to repress those negative feelings because it will make us physically ill. (Unsaved psychiatrists don't understand that we don't have to have bad feelings, because we have Someone to give them to the minute we realize we have them.)

Guess what! You are in the majority. Almost everyone grew up in a critical and negative atmosphere. The world stinks of that flavor. You can sit at Mayo Clinic waiting to get in and hear people all around you griping because they don't want to wait for their appointments. They could have come with things to do. They could write letters, read books or visit with the multitude who are there. Why do they sit there and gripe when they have the privilege of having the best medical care this world can provide? Think how some of our missionaries on foreign field—who don't even have a nurse, much less a doctor—would enjoy being able to wait for an appointment in a place like Mayo Clinic. They'd be glad to sit any length of time in order to have this type care.

One time I was to speak in Maine at a Christian Womanhood mini-spectacular. We had to change planes in New Jersey. There we took People's Express Airlines to Maine. The tickets for the two of us were less than half of what they would have cost on another airline.

People were standing around in New Jersey griping because they had to wait eight minutes for the next shuttle bus to take them across the field to get to the terminal where they were to catch their connecting flights. They could have been saying, on the flip-side, "Hey! I'm going from Chicago to Maine for a little over $150."

I couldn't help thinking how long it took people to go that far before there were planes. What about before there were even roads? That's thinking on the flip-side instead of saying, "I don't know if we should walk or wait the eight minutes." I guess they just liked to gripe. Waiting for eight minutes wouldn't have made them late for their connecting flights anyway. But they surely didn't know anything about Philippians 4:8: "Finally, brethren, whatsoever things are true, whatsoever things are honest, whatsoever things are just, whatsoever things are pure, whatsoever things are lovely, whatsoever things are of good report; if there be any virtue, if there be any praise, think on these things."

If someone says something good around you about someone else, jot it down and pass it on. **Be a gossip of good reports.** Pass on everything good you can think of, to as many people as you can, as fast as you can. That's flip-side thinking!

Learning to turn to the flip-side of life doesn't come easily. It takes practice, prayer and perseverance. Dwelling on the flip-side may be as difficult to attain as losing weight. And it's every bit as difficult to maintain! Hard to attain and hard to maintain!

As soon as we think we have attained, things begin to happen that we consider bad and we begin listing them. We go around saying to any listener, "Boy, you should have been at my house today! My washer broke down, the kids came home from school with the flu, my daughter's boy friend broke up with her, I forgot to take the meat out to thaw for supper; and then when I finally got it cooked, my husband was two hours late because he had to work late, and the food was awful anyway." You go around giving your lists. Of course, you are thinking on the bad side, so you will not be a happy, victorious Christian.

Someone once said, "When life gives you a lemon, make some lemonade!" That's a good way to tell someone to do flip-side thinking. Besides, sometimes when I have thought life was giving me lemons, it turned out that they weren't lemons after all. God brings things into our lives for good that may not seem good to us at first.

Here's another thought. Proverbs 18:22 says, "Whoso findeth a wife findeth a good thing, and obtaineth favour of the Lord." Therefore, you think marriage is God's plan for everyone—but you can't seem to find the man God has for you. So you think you are unwanted, an unclaimed blessing and all that junk. You dwell on people teasing you about it. You believe people think you are not much because you are not married.

But something we refuse to consider is that maybe God doesn't have marriage in His plan for your life (although there are those who marry for the first time in their fifties and sixties). If you have thought that, then you wonder why.

But have you also considered that the Bible says that those who are unmarried care more about how they can please the Lord, simply because their lives are not complicated by personal relationships? First Corinthians 7:32-34 says:

"But I would have you without carefulness. He that is unmarried careth for the things that belong to the Lord, how he may please the Lord: But he that is married careth for the things that are of the world, how he may please his wife. There is difference also between a wife and a virgin. The unmarried woman careth for the things of the Lord, that she may be holy both in body and in spirit: but she that is married careth for the things of the world, how she may please her husband."

If you are unmarried, think of your assets. To name just a few: your time is more your own, your money is more your own, and you don't have to please anyone with your time or money but the Lord. A married woman has more demands on both her time and money.

But if you get married, then you should think on the assets of marriage.

I had a secretary who didn't marry until she was in her thirties. She dated many men during her dating years, yet she enjoyed being single. But when the man for her came along, she had to begin thinking about the pros of married life. This type thinking will cause you to be a happy person, and you will have a satisfying, rewarding life. Turn to the flip-side!

Some people, if they had been there during Creation, would have argued with God every day when He created something and pronounced it good. They would have said, "Now that you have made light, it looks so empty here." They do reverse flip-side thinking. No matter what is good, they can figure out the corresponding bad.

When He made the sun, they would have said it was too bright; when He made the moon, they would have said it wasn't bright enough; and when He made the stars, they wouldn't have liked the way they were arranged in the heavens.

You know it's true! We are all that way to some degree. We get the house painted, and then we think we need new furniture. Then when we get new furniture, we think we need new carpet. Never, never satisfied. Our tendency is to think on the wrong side of the record.

In the summer we want it colder; in the winter we want it warmer. The spring doesn't last long enough; and the fall isn't good this year because the rain didn't come at the right time to make the trees as pretty as they usually are. But even when the majority of the trees aren't just to our liking, there are still some pretty ones out there. Go find them! Don't major on the bad ones. When you do flip-side thinking, you can actually forget to talk about the negative stuff.

I know this is difficult! I have had times when I have gone backwards in it myself. Right after chemotherapy, I did some very negative thinking. It seemed as if the drugs just took my mind and played havoc with it. It seemed there was nothing I could do to "flip it." The negative thoughts came and stayed.

Now, looking back on the experience, I think there must have been something I could have done. But, at the time, even after trying everything I knew to try, still it seemed I couldn't do flip-side thinking.

I feel sorry for those of you who have been plagued with negative thinking all your life. It's a terrible way to live. To change the way you think will take hard, hard work and much practice.

Matthew 12:35 and 36 says, "A good man out of the good treasure of the heart bringeth forth good things: and an evil man out of the evil treasure bringeth forth evil things. But I say unto you, That every idle word that men shall speak, they shall give account thereof in the day of judgment."

Every idle word about people, places, things or situations that you didn't like will be judged! God has allowed these things in our lives. Therefore, when we start griping, complaining, whining and carrying on, we're griping against God for allowing these things to happen.

My pastor, Dr. Jack Hyles, preached a sermon once entitled, "Who in the World Happened to You?" He meant that when we act or think wrongly, it is usually because we have gotten around people who have caused us to act or think that way. They are talking negatively all the time and, picking it up, we go down.

I was thinking it sure would be something if we could be the person who "happened" to someone else to influence them to be happy and good, the type person who causes others to look at the good in life.

We can't allow others to decide how we will act, but others surely do have an influence on us. God means for it to be this way according to all He says in Proverbs about people to be around and people to avoid.

Proverbs 11:27 says, "He that diligently seeketh good procureth favour: but he that seeketh mischief, it shall come unto him." Psalm 119:71 says, "It is good for me that I have been afflicted; that I might learn thy statutes."

When I first began having back trouble, that was my verse. I had always been a very active, physical person and wanted everyone else to get in there and do their part, too. But I realized it was good for me to see what it was like to be forced by poor health to stay on my back all the time. I learned a little bit about waiting for people to wait on me. It was good for my patience. And there were many other things I learned through that time. Lamentations 3:27 tells us, "It is good for a man that he bear the yoke in his youth."

You should thank God for the things that seem bad; and oftentimes the things that seem to be bad turn out for good. Let's look at a few examples.

Let's say you are a young lady who has been engaged a couple of years. Then all of a sudden, for whatever reason, there is a broken engagement. Your heart is crushed. I believe in stages of acceptance when there has been a tragedy. I think some people go through them more quickly than others—perhaps so quickly they don't even realize they have been through them—but I think there is denial, anger, depression and finally acceptance.

You know, you can go through these stages more quickly if you have learned flip-side thinking. Of course you are hurt! You will need to talk to the Lord and perhaps your parents and/or some close counselor. But to keep on talking to everyone long after the incident is over, to keep asking what you did wrong and keep dwelling on what you did wrong instead of flipping it, is wrong. You should say, *Evidently that man wasn't for me. There are some things I haven't been able to do since I've been engaged because of lack of time. I can do them now.* That's flip-side thinking!

Perhaps the washer breaks down. Now you are probably not going to jump up and down with glee. But you can call the repairman instead of sitting around commiserating with a friend about what in the world you are going to do with all the dirty laundry.

Make a happening over getting to go to the laundromat. Take along something you like to read. If you don't have transportation, wash out by hand the clothes you have to have now, and be glad about the extra time you have.

Do something you want to do that you wouldn't have had time for otherwise. Then you and the kids won't all be waiting in line at the door when your husband comes home to tell him about your rotten day—all because a machine broke down. Many men probably feel that they need a relaxing break before they come home just to get fortified to meet all the griping they will hear when they walk in the door. If you have flip-side thinking, it will make your life better and everyone in your family will be much happier.

Maybe you get up one day looking forward to doing something really exciting you have planned for a long time—a ladies' meeting, a garage sale, a Women's Missionary Society luncheon or Christmas shopping. However, you get up to find your child running a high fever and vomiting all over the place. So you say, "O Lord, no, not today. Any day but today. O God, why me??!!"

But instead of going on that way and calling every lady who was going with you and telling her all your woes, just flip it and say, "I can go out another day. Lord willing, if I live a normal life span, there will be many days I won't have a sick child at home to cuddle, rock, play with and read to—there will be many days I can do those things."

It all depends on whether or not you want to be happy. Happy people find ways to be happy. They learn flip-side thinking!

When your husband loses his job, you can cry, call Mom and Dad and others. You can cause them all to feel bad toward your husband. Or you can say, "Honey, we have each other, the kids and the Lord; together we will find a way. I believe there are several things I can do to save money." Perhaps you can bring up an idea he had in the past about starting a business of his own. Suggest this might be a good time to launch it. It all depends on your attitude—good report or bad report thinking.

It's not fun; it gets tiresome. There was a two-year period in my life during which I had five operations, chemotherapy and all the resultant tests that go along with these things. It seemed that I was going to doctors every time I turned around.

If I had let it, it could have really gotten me down. But when I did flip-side thinking, I started thinking about the orthopedically handicapped children I used to teach. Those kids had been in and out of more hospitals by the age of six than I had been by the time I was fifty. Their parents lived in doctors' offices. They also spent a lot of time in Easter Seal offices and financial aid offices trying to get money for the care their children needed. And when I got to thinking about some of those kids, I found it hard to think I had much at all wrong with me.

It's just flip-side thinking, and you have to practice it day after day, hour after hour, minute after minute.

Okay, young lady, so the boy you like doesn't like you. You have seen him with someone else. That happened to me once in college. I went to the window and stared out while I pictured the two of them together. I cried and cried and cried. Everyone came by and asked what was wrong. Silly me told them, so I'm sure it got back to him.

Of course those things hurt! The rejection hurts more than anything—our false pride has been hurt. But what we should do is go to some private place and get the crying over with, then go out to help someone else.

If he doesn't want you, he must not be the one God has for you. There must be someone better suited to you. Don't say, *He isn't any good anyway.* That's not what I mean; but God has someone better suited to you.

One year in Hyles-Anderson College chapel a prayer request was read from a woman who said, "Please pray that my white count will go up enough so I can have chemotherapy in time to come to the Spectacular." That touched me because I understood exactly what she was going through. I knew the disappointment of having to wait for a chemotherapy treatment because the white count wasn't high enough. I knew what she'd have to go through when she did have that next treatment, yet she was praying that she could have chemotherapy in time to come and sit through a long meeting!

I did hurt for her, but I also had to practice some flip-side thinking—and the flip-side was, *Hey! She wants to come to the*

Spectacular. She still has enough 'spizerinctum' to be asking for prayer for that next treatment. She's not down and out for the last count; she's not refusing to take another treatment, so she's okay yet.

My daughter had a rough first year of marriage. My husband and I didn't have any health problems or anything like that for many years after we were married. But during her first year as a wife, she had a disease that meant treatments that were difficult on her. And she didn't feel good much of the time.

She and Jeff were in missionary training camp in Missouri, which was no picnic. But she practiced flip-side thinking, and I was so thrilled. And I too had to practice flip-side thinking at that time. Instead of thinking, *Boy, it's really hard on her,* I had to think, *Jeff's staying right by and helping her through all this sickness, boot camp and jungle camp—which is really difficult in itself. God knows they need all this in their first year of marriage—just like He knew exactly when my husband and I would need it in our lives.*

Practice flip-side thinking!

Luke 6:45 says, "A good man out of the good treasure of his heart bringeth forth that which is good; and an evil man out of the evil treasure of his heart bringeth forth that which is evil: for of the abundance of the heart his mouth speaketh." Do you want to speak right and be right? Then you will have to flip it! This subject is so much like looking for redbirds and watching trees. I guess I'm trying to find a different way to say it so that it might reach someone whom redbirds and trees won't reach.

There is so much negative and bad in this world today—why even think about it? Why dwell on it, even if it is true? Have good report thinking instead. It will cause you to have a happier life, no matter what situation you are in.

It is something that won't happen overnight. You have to practice it and do it over and over again. Anyone can find the bad in things. God can help us see the flip side: Psalm 4:7 says, "Thou hast put gladness in my heart, more than in the time that their corn and their wine increased."

When I was feeling so bad after chemotherapy, the pastor of the 37th Street Baptist Church in Rochester, Minnesota, wrote me a letter and said:

> The Lord has different yardsticks to measure the same people at different times. It is not the same when he or she is a teenager or a young adult or a mature leader or an older adult. And here's the case in point. It's not the same measure or yardstick when we are sick, afflicted or laid aside in some way. Just simply operating at twenty to thirty percent may, in fact, be a great victory in sickness, when in full health it would have been laziness and tragic waste of time and talent.

Are you sick? Are you laid aside? If the answer is "yes," then are you operating at twenty to thirty percent? If so, then thank God for that! Flip it! Don't say, "But I used to do. . . ." Say, "I am doing. . . ." Don't say, "But I have so much yet to do." Say, "I am getting this done." Don't judge yourself; let the Lord do it. And certainly don't let others do it. First Corinthians 4:1-5 has some good verses for you to claim:

"Let a man so account of us, as of the ministers of Christ, and stewards of the mysteries of God. Moreover it is required in stewards, that a man be found faithful. But with me it is a very small thing that I should be judged of you, or of man's judgment: yea, I judge not mine own self. For I know nothing by myself; yet am I not hereby justified: but he that judgeth me is the Lord. Therefore judge nothing before the time, until the Lord come, who both will bring to light the hidden things of darkness, and will make manifest the counsels of the hearts: and then shall every man have praise of God."

So, you are never satisfied; you are on the wrong side of the record:

"I sure do wish it weren't so hot."

"Oh, it's too cold for me."

"I think I'd rather be out West."

"I dream of Tennessee."
"Do you know what she said to me?"
"Why does she never speak?"
"He acts like such a big macho man—but men are all so weak."
"Just when I need her, she's not there."
"She never leaves me be!"
"Why do they leave me all alone?"
"I need some privacy."
"Mom checks up on me all the time."
"My mom doesn't seem to care what I do."
"God is always 'getting onto' me!"
"It seems as if God doesn't even know I exist."
"I just don't have a thing to wear."
"This closet is just too small."
"I am just too short!"
"I fear I'm much too tall."
"Why did God make me like this?"
"Why can't she be like me?"
"I wish they'd do it like I want."
"I just can't see it her way!"

It doesn't matter how things go,
We'll not be satisfied;
Our pity parties will go on
Until we all have died.
But maybe there is still some hope:
If we were not so blind,
God could point out a world of good
With which to fill our minds.

—Mary Purdum

Flip-side thinking. Do you want to be happy? Fulfilled? Get into Matthew chapter 5—I call them "The Blesseds." Blessed means "happy, fulfilled, contented and joyous." Do you want to be that kind of person? You say, "That's just not the kind of personality I have." It's not anyone's personality! All of us have to learn how to be that way! It just depends on how you look at life and how much you really want to change your thinking to the positive side of things.

Let's all do some flip-side thinking!

24 – How to Rejoice in the Lord Through Problem Times

How do you really rejoice in the Lord always?

"Always" includes so many different situations: death, sickness, financial problems, unemployment, hunger, homesickness, children failing you or seeming to fail themselves. It could go on and on.

Rejoicing in the Lord always takes some real doing. But our God is so wonderful that He didn't just tell us to rejoice in the Lord always; He goes ahead and tells us how to rejoice in the Lord always. In Philippians 4:8 we are told to rejoice in those things that are honest, just, lovely, pure, true and of good report. And a lot of people do know how to rejoice in the Lord always.

Speaking of always rejoicing, let me tell you about someone who does it. Her name is Ruth Ann. She had twenty-five operations by the time she was ten. When she was ten, I asked her when her last operation took place. She couldn't tell me, though it had been only a few months ago. She said she "didn't count because keeping surgery dates wasn't important to her."

When asked what made her happy when she had to go in for surgery, she said she liked getting I.V.'s early when she went in because then they didn't have to use the mask when it was time for surgery.

Talk about rejoicing in the good! I'd say those are pretty good examples, wouldn't you? She has a zest for life that many of us do not have.

I sometimes wonder if many of us don't need a whole lot of sicknesses. It seems that as soon as much sickness comes, we begin to realize what life is about and what we should major on in life. As Ruth Ann says, "I don't think about my surgery dates." She doesn't dwell on them. She decides what she will think on—and that secret most fifty-year-olds don't know.

Because she was born with spina bifida, Ruth Ann is probably way ahead of most adults when it comes to rejoicing through problems. She is a joy and blessing to everyone who knows her. She is a good example of how we can learn to rejoice in the Lord always.

I am so tired of hearing, "Well, I could learn to rejoice in the Lord if. . . ." There is no "I could rejoice in the Lord if. . ." at all. It is through problems that we learn to rejoice.

When you stop to think that one out of every two or three marriages will end in divorce and one out of two or three will have cancer (and that's only two things that seem to blight our lives—there are many more), you can see there will be problems to face.

Some people say, "Why even talk about it?" Because it's life! Death is universal. And before you die, you don't know what else you will have to face. But it's not bad or fatalistic when you think of it in the right way; when you realize the Lord will be with you through whatever happens.

Nahum 1:7 tells us, "The Lord is good, a strong hold in the day of trouble; and he knoweth them that trust in him."

Psalm 118:24 says, "This is the day which the Lord hath made; we will rejoice and be glad in it."

Look at Psalm 119:71: "It is good for me that I have been afflicted; that I might learn thy statutes."

Some of you young people haven't had too many troubles. Are you wondering how you will ever be able to go through problems?

The wonderful thing about it is, you are not to sit and ponder on that. You sit and ponder on the Lord; then He will give you the grace for whatever He allows to come into your life.

Sometimes you who have special riches need grace to handle it. You might laugh at that, but some families are terribly messed up because of too much money. The children are messed up, the parents are messed up, the whole family is messed up.

Whatever the problem may be in your life, God has the answer.

When I was just a little kid and didn't know much about the Bible, one verse I did learn was John 10:10. When our family doctor came to our house, I had him sign his name in my autograph book. (I had never heard of putting a Scripture with your name, but he did it.) He signed John 10:10, which says, "The thief cometh not, but for to steal, and to kill, and to destroy: I am come that they might have life, and that they might have it more abundantly."

The Lord wants us to have an abundant life, a full life, a life of joy, love, peace, satisfaction and happiness. He teaches us how to have it and then gives us all we need in order to have it.

One summer I was sitting in the sand messing around. I built a castle and put a moat around it. All of a sudden God seemed to speak to me: "Marlene, that's how I have you protected. You are in the middle, and there is a circle of protection around you. I will always be there, and you can use anything I give you for that circle of protection for whatever you have to go through."

It was a wonderfully sweet lesson to me. I realized that He has given me hundreds of people who care for me and for whom I care. He's given me thousands of trees to love, and I enjoy them so much.

The other day I asked our college gardener to check on a sick tree. (He asked me if I wanted him to lay hands on it! I told him I didn't care as long as he fixed it!) It's right in front of my house. If it were to die, it would leave a big gap in my circle of protection. I love trees, birds, sunrises, sunsets. Nature is very much a part of my circle of protection. But some of you don't even notice things like that.

One morning as my husband and I were coming home from our regular breakfast outing, we backtracked several blocks just to see a badger. It's wonderful to start a day enjoying God's creations. But some of you don't enjoy God's nature—even thinking it's foolish to do so. But we need everything we can get in our circle of protection, especially in this day.

The world is full of good things, but there are bad things, too. The worldly system is terrible; but the world God made still has so many very beautiful things. Take all that He gives you and use it to fight against going along with the worldly system.

We need exciting lives. If you live a dull life, there will be a very big temptation to go over to the worldly system to get the wrong type of things for your excitement.

Get excited over sunrises and sunsets, birds on the wing and squirrels hiding nuts. It's all so much fun to watch if you decide you are going to like it.

God has also given us work. What a marvelous thing it is! Years ago someone told me about a lady they knew who had lost her son. She said folks criticized this woman because the day after the funeral she came home and started rewallpapering her house. But I thought it was wonderful that God had given her work as a part of her circle of protection. Some people can vent their hurt, frustration and anger on wallpaper instead of having a pity party or lashing out at someone else. Work can be such a blessing if you organize it right and don't get yourself overly fatigued.

He gave us all kinds of activities. You who are fairly young—the older people, too—learn now everything you can of that which God would approve. Don't make fun of anyone else's fun.

If someone is a bird-watcher (I love birds, but I won't sit in the rain all day looking for a particular type bird), don't make fun of him. Maybe that's part of his circle of protection.

Some women love to quilt. People will say, "Go buy a quilt. You could spend your time on better things." But that person may need to quilt. It might be a part of her circle of protection.

Some men who don't have to work for income after they retire may need to do woodworking, or something else, as part of their circle of protection.

One summer we visited a family where the man had retired. I had never seen him so happy. He was in his back yard stripping different pieces of furniture and refinishing them for very little money. His wife was saying, "I don't know why he does this." He needed to do it because he was achieving something and enjoyed seeing something beautiful come out of what he did. He didn't need the money as much as he needed the circle of protection.

You know what happens to many folks who retire? They sit down and stay sitting down. Then they rot, and then they die. Hence, it is very important to have a circle of protection that will take you through whatever problems you may face.

It's very possible that you will have to bring your circle of protection into play following some tragedy in life. Suppose you develop multiple sclerosis and can't drive or walk or see. But perhaps you can hear. Have you developed good listening habits so that you can listen to all kinds of good tapes if something like this happens to you?

If you don't like to read, learn! Even if you have to start with Snoopy, learn! Get some help. Perhaps your eyes will be with you when the rest of your body ceases to function. If you live long enough, you go out of this world the same way you came in—toothless, hairless, etc. So throughout life you are losing. And the more you lose, the more you need to have in your circle of protection.

If you have an adequate circle of protection, you will never feel deprived. You will not be like the old ladies in the nursing homes who are constantly bemoaning the fact that no one ever comes to visit them. You will be one of those cheerful ones like a lady my dad goes to see in Arapahoe, Nebraska, who's well over one hundred. Every year she has something else she's doing. Perhaps she's making a new quilt for one of her kids. She has something to be excited about that year. That's a "young" person—one who has something she is excited about.

If you have a child for whom school is difficult, just begin helping him achieve a little bit in his weak subjects. It can be done, and that thing will one day be a part of his circle of protection.

My circle of protection makes me feel so special—as if God is so wonderful. My husband is a part of my circle of protection, but let's say he dies. (You know what happens to a close couple when one dies. The remaining partner will often fall to pieces. It has nothing to do with how much the partner was loved; it has to do with the fact that the remaining partner keeps his/her eyes on the gap in the circle. That one continues to dwell on the death, and all he/she sees is the gap.) If my husband should pass away, I could still be aware of the gap while going on to concentrate on other things in my circle of protection. Perhaps I could go on to Scripture verses. Let's say I go on to Romans 8:35-39. Instead of looking just at the gap left by my husband's death, I could focus on this:

"Who shall separate us from the love of Christ? shall tribulation, or distress, or persecution, or famine, or nakedness, or peril, or sword? As it is written, For thy sake we are killed all the day long; we are accounted as sheep for the slaughter. Nay, in all these things we are more than conquerors through him that loved us. For I am persuaded, that neither death, nor life, nor angels, nor principalities, nor powers, nor things present, nor things to come, Nor height, nor depth, nor any other creature, shall be able to separate us from the love of God, which is in Christ Jesus our Lord."

It's kind of hard to be "down in the mouth" when you are dwelling on being more than conquerors and the fact that nothing can separate us from the love of God. I could look at the verses and perhaps glance back at the gap without getting my full attention on it and say, "Lord, nothing can separate me from You—not even my husband's death. He even pointed me to You while he was living."

So I could keep on living. I would miss him, and there would be tears; but I could smile through the tears because I had some verses to lean on. I could go outside and look at a tree instead of sitting inside moping. I could even enjoy some of the trees I enjoyed with my husband when he lived. Now I might even cry under the tree, but I would not sorrow as those who have no hope. There would be a joy in my heart along with the sorrow. And that is a healthy way of sorrowing.

Perhaps I could call a friend in the middle of the night (if she had no one living with her whom I might disturb) to pray with me when I couldn't get victory over negative thoughts. I wouldn't even have to tell her, "I'm having a terrible time." All I'd need to say would be, "I can't get in the Bible for myself. Can you read it to me and pray with me?"

Then let's say I lost my daughter right after I lost my husband. (This does happen to people.) I wouldn't be able to handle this unless I looked around at the circle of protection God had given me. So losing a daughter I would have two gaps in my circle of protection. But because I had already fortified myself well with a large circle of protection, I would still have plenty of places within my circle to turn when I had another gap to face.

That's why we should fortify ourselves now even if nothing has happened to us yet. We never know when we will need that circle of protection.

Scripture verses are a part of my circle. Psalm 23 is one of my special ones. There's also John 14:1-7. Find the ones that mean the most to you.

Just as an example, let me tell you a little bit more about my circle of protection. Perhaps it will give you ideas about things to add to your own.

I love oak trees, Nancy Perry, strawberries and my preacher. Then there are redbirds and my dad. My mom's out of my circle now; but I have what she left me as far as teaching and training, and I have my memories of her. I like Queen Anne's Lace, *The Joyful Woman* magazine, maple trees and the United States of America. I love Deep River Park and my children, Joy and David. I love Jeff Ryder and Cathe Evans, my son-in-law and daughter-in-law, and Jordan Ryder, my grandson.

I love weeping willow trees. I used to play under them as a child so when I see them, I look at them, enjoy them and talk about them.

I like Annie Ruth McGuire (a friend from Chattanooga, Tennessee), sunsets, little bunnies, Lake Michigan, Philippians 4:4-8 and my niece, Beth Emory. I like goldfinches and Diane Smith, my niece. I like lilacs, Mom and Dad Evans, the *Reader's Digest* and Philippians 3:10.

I love the Great Smoky Mountains, Hyles-Anderson students and Isaiah 1:18. I like to write and I like to read. And I love Mike Smith and Jim Emory, my nephews. I love the Romans Road, my sister, Catherine Emory, Proverbs 31; and I like my house, "Clair de Lune," lilies of the valley, azaleas and quilts.

I like the feeling of afghans on a fall day and fireplaces and pumpkins. I like the color of peppers—the brilliant red and the brilliant green. And I like the textures of materials. I like boys and girls, men and women and little babies—I just like people!

I like poached eggs and Tennessee and childhood stories. I like JoJo Moffitt and memories of Bob Jones University.

I like Mrs. Beverly Hyles, the Dr. Lee Robersons, Nebraska, snow on pine and fur trees, popcorn, greeting cards and biographies.

I like to counsel and to live for other people. I love Dick Emory and Jerry Smith, my brothers-in-law; the staff and faculty of

Hyles-Anderson College and my sister, Doris Smith. I could list at least ten thousand other things, people and situations that are a part of my circle of protection.

Now your circle of protection will be different. For example, at the age of thirty-five anything that involved much physical activity left my circle of protection. I used to love to shop just to get ideas, and now I can't; but you might have that as a big part of your circle.

You know, if I had just shut my mouth and kept my body still as a child, I would have more in my circle of protection than I have. I could have had piano lessons, because my folks had the money and were going to sacrifice to see that I had them. I could have had quilting, sewing, embroidering, tatting and many other handcrafts because my mom knew how to do them and wanted to teach me. But I wouldn't sit still long enough to learn.

I "won" then—but I have lost out now! Everything you don't learn will cause you to be a loser. Anything you can possibly put into your circle of protection, get it there.

I have heard so many people say, "I just sit down and play the piano for my own enjoyment. It soothes me." Oh, I wish I could do that! I just love to hear a good pianist play, but I don't have that in my circle. I can't worry about it now, because I don't have time to change it. But maybe later I can add it—it is never too late to add to your circle!

My circle of protection is also different from that of a younger person, and that is fine! But be sure you have a circle!

Some of you have sports in your circle, like skiing, hiking, backpacking or white-water rafting. Keep those things in your circle as long as possible. When I lost the physical activity side of my circle, it left a big gap. So now I have to really keep my eyes on the things I can do! If I dwelt on the loss of physical activity, I could go to pieces.

Each of us has something we could go to pieces over—maybe

a background full of problems, a lack of education, sickness in a family, not achieving goals we want to achieve, physical illness or whatever. The idea is to keep your eyes on another part of your circle.

It's your decision. You can lose your faith in one friend or a preacher. You can lose sight of your whole life because you lose the ability to do physical things. You can declare your life over because of a tragedy (like losing a parent or spouse). *Or* you can say, "There's a gap that will never be filled, but I'll turn and turn to see all that God has given me for a circle of protection." And *that's* going to determine whether or not you learn to really rejoice in the Lord through problems.

Develop your circle now—before you lose your job, your daughter, a friend, your eyes or your confidence in a full-time Christian worker. It's the way to really "rejoice in the Lord alway."

When this chapter came to me to be proofread, I just "happened" to be in bed taking it easy after a mastectomy. As I proofread, my heart thrilled with joy as I realized that the Lord had been preparing me for a loss through cancer. I had no qualms or fears; I only had gratefulness to the Lord that He had already been working in my body. The doctor told me at the time of the surgery that the cancer had probably been present in my body at least a year.

The same week that I proofread this chapter, I got a letter from someone who said, "Your 'rejoice in the Lord alway' thing won't work." Yes, it will! I've tried it and I know. I can say again and again that God gives a circle of protection.

I shed a few tears over God's goodness to me during my bout with cancer. But as far as I know, I didn't shed a tear or lose a moment's sleep over the cancer itself. I didn't even have to take a sleeping pill to get to sleep the night before the surgery, because I had a circle of protection and God had already been preparing me.

Before surgery the doctor said, "I don't think we will have to do a mastectomy." But the Lord had already told me they would have to do one. So when the doctor came in after surgery, he didn't have to tell me—I told him. God had already been preparing me. I was able to cope with the treatments and medications that I took after the surgery because of my circle of protection.

I'm not saying I will never have problems with rejoicing through problems. If I were to get cancer again and have to suffer like some people I've known, I have no idea how I'd respond. I just know that, up to this point, my circle of protection has always worked. No one is going to tell me it can't. I know that there are high-powered medicines that can make people say and do things that can't be controlled. But I do know that for normal situations, a circle of protection will help us through bad and trying circumstances.

You know, God's grace is sufficient. A week after my mastectomy I was scheduled to be in a mini-spectacular in Tampa, Florida. Many people whom I love in my circle of protection made it possible for me to be in that meeting. They stayed with me at O'Hare airport until my plane left. When I landed in Tampa, they saw that the plane was met with a wheelchair so as to preserve my strength.

When I got to the meeting, I thought I would just be able to make an appearance. But they made me so comfortable that I was able to be there for quite awhile. The preacher's recliner was on the platform for me. Someone did my hair and makeup. As a result of all of this care from people in my circle of protection, I was able to do all of my scheduled teaching.

This is what God means when He says, "My grace is sufficient." The reason God's grace is not sufficient for some of you is that you are not taking advantage of what He gives you. You don't have to be down in the mouth about anything.

As I said before, there are times when people aren't themselves because of certain medications. These medical situations are excluded from what I'm discussing. Other than these medical situations, no situation in life should cause us to stop rejoicing. It is as simple as learning to enjoy the things God has given instead of just passing by them.

People tell me some women completely fall apart after a mastectomy. Those are the ones who have counted only on one thing in life—their physical appearance. They feel less than a woman if one portion of the body has been mutilated. But if you have a circle of protection, you know that one small part of your body being taken away will not make you any less of a person. That someone would get depressed and question God over this kind of surgery is worldly thinking. We might question God why He hasn't let more happen to us!

After surgery, some people warned me that I would begin questioning God. Had I done so, I would have been sinning—unless I questioned Him about what He wanted to teach me by this experience. But this, "O God, why me" stuff! Why not me! I am a sinner saved by grace just like you. And according to my Bible, sickness is for a lot of things besides punishing sin.

If we could only learn to go to the Bible and take advantage of our circle of protection, nothing would bother us. I'm not proud that I didn't fall apart; I'm just thankful that His grace is sufficient. It has been sufficient for half a century and more; why won't it be sufficient for the rest of my life?

It can be sufficient for you, too—that is, if you start making that circle deep and thick and big. Make it as deep as possible. Bring in every good thing possible. Learn to like things you don't now like—they could mean so much to you later on.

You can rejoice in the Lord always—through problems.

"Rejoice in the Lord alway: and again I say, Rejoice." It will work!

25 – Is Your Life Changed?

Romans 12:1 and 2 says:

"I beseech you therefore, brethren, by the mercies of God, that ye present your bodies a living sacrifice, holy, acceptable unto God, which is your reasonable service. And be not conformed to this world: but be ye transformed by the renewing of your mind, that ye may prove what is that good, and acceptable, and perfect, will of God."

". . . by the renewing of your mind." At the end of this chapter you will be hearing about some people whose lives were changed. They had to be, in order to do some of the things they have done to help us through the ages. There are Bible women, women who have meant something to me personally, and women from history. I mixed them all up—there is no chronological order. But each has come to me at a time when I needed the example of her life to inspire and encourage me.

I want to know if perhaps you don't want a changed life. We all know we are not happy if we are not changing. People must be doing something a little better or a little faster, or they are not fulfilled or challenged. They are not living a dynamic life.

We hear about victorious Christian living, but most of us do not have it. We don't have a testimony before the world because we are just about as upset as the world. We have not had that renewing of our minds.

If you have to iron today, find a better, more efficient way to iron. Decide to learn Scripture while you iron those shirts. Decide to cut down on the amount of time it usually takes you to iron those shirts. Do something to make life a challenge.

Some of you are asking, "What about this changed life? Can I find a woman who will help me to be different?"

Those of you who have been around me very much know that I believe one woman can be used to change the life of another. So I often ask, "Who's your lady?" Some of you say, "I don't have a lady."

We get letters at the *Christian Womanhood* office from those who ask, "Do you know someone in my area to whom I could go?" I probably wouldn't know the woman God wants you to have.

As an example: let's say you don't know how to do housework, so you work at everything else besides housework. You go soul winning twenty hours a week so you can say, "I just can't keep house like other women because I'm out soul winning so much."

You are letting your good be "evil spoken of" because you need to have a balanced life. Romans 14:16 says, "Let not then your good be evil spoken of." You need to go soul winning, but you also need to know how to keep house. Most of you are not lazy: you just haven't been taught how to keep a house. So you need a lady in your life to teach you.

But what lady wants to go to another and say, "You know, I have never learned how to dust and vacuum. I've never learned that there are some daily jobs, some weekly jobs and some seasonal jobs." You won't admit that the reason you keep so busy at other things is that you don't know how to keep your house.

Then there are those who won't admit they don't know how to go soul winning. And you won't go out and find a lady who can teach you. So what do you do? You worship your house, cleaning it when it is already clean. You bake and cook, and bake some more, when your family would be better off without the extra sweets. Then you say, "I just can't do all that work at the church because taking care of my home and family is a full-time job." When translated, this is what you mean: "I don't know how to go soul winning, so I'll keep myself so busy that I can say I don't have time to go."

Why don't we just confess our faults to one another, as James 5:16 commands: "Confess your faults one to another, and pray one for another"? Why don't we ask for help? If you don't know one lady who "has her act together" in many areas, perhaps you will have to have a circle of ladies. You may have to get help with your housecleaning from one whose soul-winning habits you wouldn't like to imitate. But if you hang around her a bit, she might be the lady for whom you are looking.

So many times if a lady sees you are looking to her, she will become a better person.

Some of you have heard me say that Elaine Colsten says that every time someone says something nice about her, she runs home and becomes that really fast before people know she isn't that.

This, too, could happen to your lady. If you begin to appreciate one area in her life, she may begin to say, "Oh, I had better watch it!"

That has happened to me. Girls in the college where I work look to me, and sometimes I think, *Oh, they can't look to me in that area. I'd better work on that.*

As you choose the woman or circle of women God has for you, you may be the one who sees to it that she or they become even better because of your praise of certain areas in their lives.

Another way you can get a woman in your life is to be that woman in someone else's life. You argue: "I couldn't do that. There's nothing that different about me. What could anyone get from me?"

Maybe the desire to be different. You see, so few women even want to change, who will even admit they need to change, who even want to add to their lives, want to grow. But if you will even admit that, you might be the very one who could be something to a girl. You might be the cause of her saying, "I see her still growing. I see that she can still admit her faults. Therefore, I can, too."

Perhaps she can even learn from you as she sees you struggling against certain temptations. Remember I Corinthians 10:13: "There hath no temptation taken you but such as is common to man; but God is faithful, who will not suffer you to be tempted above that ye are able; but will with the temptation also make a way to escape, that ye may be able to bear it."

Be an example in how you watch for the escape route, how you flee from the devil, how you see to it that you are not around those things to which you know you could yield because you are weak in that certain area. Why not be an example to some girls and show them how God is helping you?

Many of you have been so kind to the ladies here at First Baptist Church in Hammond and Hyles-Anderson College. You say, "Isn't that a great bunch of ladies!"

We do have some great ladies; and you also have some of those "great ladies" in your own church, but you overlook them since they are "right under your nose."

Do you realize that we have people coming into First Baptist Church who don't revere the ladies here as much as you who consider them to be great women of God? Don't you know that an "expert" has to come from at least fifty miles away!

But the women at First Baptist are just women striving toward a goal, trying to be different, trying not to yield to temptation, trying to have their minds renewed through Christ.

I imagine you have some of these same kinds of ladies right around you.

Ask God to give you a lady! My heart breaks when I hear people say, "I don't have a lady because there isn't a lady." I have begun to say to some of you, "Come on; let's get a circle of ladies.

Let's learn from different ones. Let's ask God to help us become complete as we get one thing from one and something else from another. Oh, that we would ask God to help us do this!

Some of you are so sunk in the thought, *This is just the way I am,* that you are never going to see Him do anything through you because you have decided there is nothing that can be done.

Perhaps you have decided that your marriage has failed—that it's gone. You don't love your husband anymore, and nothing can change it. Aw, c'mon! What is this stuff about not loving your husband anymore? Whomever you put your mind on and whomever you think toward—that's who you love!

Start doing for that husband and act as if you love him; and do you know what? You'll end up loving that husband! Yet you act like it won't be happening and couldn't possibly happen to you for a long, long time. You could fall in love with your husband *today* if you would put your mind on him and pray for him and think on the good things he does instead of on the bad. You could have a marriage revived today.

Oh, I know it takes time to grow in that marriage again. But it seems that the word *love* is rather thrown around. Love has a lot to do with duty. But we don't like the word *duty.* We like to say, "Love, love, love! It's just whomever you fall in love with!"

The one you need to fall in love with is your husband! And you need to ask God to give you every bit of mind control that you can muster in order to have a marriage again.

It was my privilege one time to have a woman call me and say, "You know what? We haven't had a marriage for eight or nine years. But it's different today—and it's going to be different from now on. It's not just a changed life for awhile; it's to be a changed life forever."

Then there are those who say, "Well, I don't know; I don't think I even loved him when I married him." So what? Love him now! That's the important thing.

What do you need to change? The most important thing in our

lives is to add to them. I don't mean that you should become a different person, but what or whom do you need to add to your life? Bible women? A girl you don't even like? You may need to be around her and get a bit of those things you don't even like! If she just seems to bug you, probably it is because you don't have even a little bit of what she has in abundance.

You may live in a college dorm with a girl who is so neat that it just kills you. You can't even put your coat on your bed without her saying in her sweetest voice, "Don't you want to hang it up?" You want to counter with: "As a matter of fact, I don't! If I wanted to, I would have! You see it lying there, don't you?"

Maybe that overly neat girl needs some of the girl who comes in and slings her clothes all over the place.

Because we react against one another and decide we don't want to have anything to do with each other, we are not adding to our lives.

I received another letter recently from a woman who said she would like to add some of the wisdom of Mrs. John R. Rice, some of the charm and graciousness of Mrs. Jack Hyles, some of the joy of Elaine Colsten and some of the organization of some other woman.

That's it! That's the story! Instead of fighting those who are not like you, pull from every woman around you. We have spent too much time fighting others and being catty and coy and ugly. Now let's decide to love others. Then God will be able to use us as He was able to use Mrs. Susannah Spurgeon, Mrs. Susanna Wesley, Mrs. Adoniram Judson, Mrs. Martin Luther and many others like them.

Do you think they were any different from us? I can't believe they were. I think they were just women who decided they were going to be special for Him.

Now II Corinthians 5:17 reads: "Therefore if any man be in Christ, he is a new creature: old things are passed away; behold, all things are become new."

We need to change. We don't need to become another person, but we do need to become different. I would like to see the day when women say, "You know, there's a woman in my life."

You have heard me say, "There was a woman in the church." Now wouldn't it be great if that woman were not mean and hateful but pure, lovely and joyful, a woman whom everybody wanted to be around, one everybody looked to to point her to the Lord?

That type woman we must have if America is to be saved. If our children are to become giants for God like the Wesley brothers, if we are to have husbands used of God like Charles Haddon Spurgeon, we must have women with purity, love and forgiveness. We must have women about whom people say, "I don't know what it is about her, but she is different!"

Do others say that about you? Have you decided that is what you want more than anything else? Have you decided that you want to be spiritually reproductive so girls will want to be exactly like you?

Perhaps you don't want girls and women imitating you because you know of some things in your life that aren't Christlike. But if they see Jesus in you—that's what matters.

Jesus isn't now walking on earth. We don't see Him in human form. We look in the Word and with the help of the Holy Spirit, we find what we should be doing. But we humanly represent the Lord Jesus.

Are you representing Him in a way that causes girls to want to be ladies—like you? Are you a representative who causes girls to want to say to you, "I'd love to dress the way you do. There's something different about the way you walk, the way you sit, the way you stand"? This means our manner of dress must be very special. Most of you don't have the money to go out and buy a lot of clothes. But you do have time to work on putting the right things together so you always look nice.

No matter where they are or what they are doing, Christian

women should be the ones who cause folks to ask, "Where are you going? Why are you so dressed up?"

Now I realize there are times when you need to do your cleaning, and I am not suggesting you wear your Sunday best for that. But we all should watch the length of our skirts, the way our clothes fit, the cut of our necklines, and try to fix ourselves up a bit, no matter what we have planned for the day. We should match our colors and learn all we can about dressing with our limited finances. And all this should be done in an effort to please our Lord. We should dress very carefully because we want some lives changed forever! We don't want changed lives just because of an emotional experience. In order to really captivate the hearts of some young girls and change their lives, we must be pure inside and our faces must show the radiance of that purity and our dress must reflect the Lord Jesus.

Have you ever heard a girl say about a woman, "When I look at her, I feel like I am seeing Jesus"? Let others see Jesus through you.

Jesus chose to use people. That is special. You don't need to go around wondering what you will do when your children leave home, or what you will do when you are "stuck" in the house with two or three babies in diapers and you are climbing the walls, or wondering what you will do when you retire. You can always be what the Lord wants. And as you are challenged and excited about becoming that lady, you will never feel old. Just work on having some girls and women look to you for an example.

Even if your lot in life is lying in a rest home and not being able to move anything but your lips, you can still be a blessing to others. You can pray for us who can go and do. Be someone special. If you can only move your lips in a smile, do it! Smile when someone visits you so she can say, "I went to cheer her up, but, instead, she cheered me up!"

Whether you are in a rest home or whether you are a young

mother with several kids, let God add to your life. And love women and girls as you have never loved them before!

There were some pilgrim women whose lives were changed forever. They left the comforts of nice homes to sail to a strange land, to endure hardships, disease, cold, lack of food and Indian attacks because of the faith of their husbands. I wonder if they did it willingly? It had to be hard.

Once I heard about some pilgrim ladies leaving Holland to come to this country for the freedom of Christian education for their children. Though they had some religious freedoms, they still couldn't give their children a Christian education.

Today we find those who think it is hard to leave home and family and all they have loved, just to go to another state for a Christian education for their husbands. We need women with changed lives, women who will do what it takes to see that their children have a Christian education.

On one occasion eighteen pilgrim women left their homeland to come to America. Only four lived through that first grueling winter. Surely those women had changed lives forever.

We need more like them!

I wonder if **Susanna Wesley**'s life was changed forever? She devoted her entire life to training her children to live godly. She patiently instructed each child. Susanna reared those giants of the Faith, John and Charles Wesley. She spent the prime time of her life teaching her children godliness and character. Surely her life exemplified a changed life forever.

We need more like her who will give themselves completely to seeing their children reared for God.

How about **Susannah Spurgeon**? Was her life changed forever? She missed her husband so much when he traveled. I wonder if she was really willing to become a servant to him, to suffer sickness, to be left alone, even while she was sick, to care for two small sons while her husband traveled?

So far was she from resentment that she dedicated herself to her husband's work and started a book fund to supply Spurgeon's books and messages to poor preachers. She is the one about whom her husband said, "I have served the Lord far more and never less because of your sweet companionship."

I am sure she thinks it was really worth it, now that she can look down from Heaven and see preachers all over the world receiving help from a man named Spurgeon. I imagine she has decided that it was really worth putting herself last. Hers was a changed life forever.

Is yours?

Then there was **Ann Judson**. The book I read about Adoniram Judson seemed to be so much about his wife. I read how Ann's hair fell out, yet she kept on working for the Lord without being embarrassed.

When a boy came to me and said, "Mrs. Evans, my girl friend is dying of cancer, and the treatment given her is causing her to lose her hair," I told Ann Judson's story to this young man and he told it to his girl friend. And before that young girl died, she wrote me a beautiful letter saying, "If Ann Judson could laugh about her hair falling out, so can I!"

Though Ann Judson is dead, yet she still lives. She lived in the life of a young girl who died of cancer a few years ago.

Do you think Ann enjoyed going to the jail to comfort her husband? and working fifteen hours a day to support a family? That today is inhuman according to many Christian women. Do you think she was willing to quietly accept her husband's convictions?

Yes, Ann Judson's life was changed. She was willing to suffer prison beside her husband and even go to an early grave for the work God had called her to do.

Thank you, Ann Judson, for having a changed life and for giving a sixteen-year-old girl the courage to die gracefully.

Then there is a woman without whom I would perhaps not have a ministry—**Mrs. Coystal Hyles.** I doubt there would be a First Baptist Church or a Hyles-Anderson College except for this woman. I probably would not have had the opportunity to put out a paper called *Christian Womanhood* without the support and approval of a pastor—who was her son.

I doubt if we know how much we owe Mrs. Coystal Hyles. And we will never be able to express it to her here on this earth, but she knows, now that she is in Heaven and can see her works following after her.

She faithfully cared for a sick, retarded little girl until she died at the age of seven, and that almost alone. Then she patiently cared for another sick daughter until she found her arms empty again. I just wonder how she went on. Didn't she feel it was just too much for one person to bear?

She took her fatherless son and faithfully trained him to hate sin. She trained him to look at beer and cigarette advertisements and say, "No! No! Bad! Bad!" Just because she trained him to do that, we are training our children that way today. Hers was a changed life forever.

Ruth's was a changed life. She became an obedient servant and relinquished her rights just to care for an aged mother-in-law, Naomi. That doesn't sound like much fun, does it? Wonder if she didn't have times when she wanted to do things her own way? But Ruth resigned herself completely to God's direction and worked diligently and humbly.

Because hers was a changed life, we call our daughters Ruth; we call our ladies groups the Ruth Circle.

God rewarded her with a family of her own and made her an ancestor of our Saviour. This woman gave up her rights in order to gain more than her rights.

We need more such women!

Dorcas had a changed life. She was full of good works. Oh, to have women today who deserve to have that said of them at their life's end!

Dorcas gave her time and talent to making clothes for the poor.

I wish we had some ladies now who would sew for our girls and make them modest clothing—not criticizing but spending time helping them. Oh, for women full of good works like Sister Dorcas—content to work at home without aspiring to be a leader. Surely hers was a changed life forever, winning many to Jesus because of the testimony of her sweet and giving spirit.

Esther's was a changed life. Obeying her guardian, she saved her people from destruction. Oh, that we had women who would save America from destruction! Perhaps her modest and sweet spirit helped her to win the heart of a great king, who respected her wishes. Esther was willing to risk her position—yes, her very life—to save her friends and loved ones. We need some Esthers who will risk their very lives, knowing that fear does not come from God. May we read her story, then go forth to save America in the same way—by loving our country and those around us.

Mary's was truly a changed life forever. Mary humbly submitted her all to God and accepted His will even when it meant her friends and family might not understand. Of course she was embarrassed, this precious girl in such a circumstance. Surely she cared what others thought. But she went right ahead and humbly and willingly accepted the awesome responsibility of rearing the very Son of God.

Surely Mary's life was a changed life forever.

Sabina Wurmbrand had a changed life forever. This saint endured imprisonment, beatings and heavy manual labor because of her faith in Jesus and dedication to her husband's work.

Oh, but we today would claim that heavy work is too hard for us, and we don't want to do it. And we question why she really did it.

Sabina kept up her husband's visitation schedule while he was a prisoner; surely then no one would expect her to keep up her own schedule at this time. But hers was a changed life forever and, even though she was separated from her husband and child for four years, even though she also became a prisoner, Sabina never pitied herself nor gave in to depression or discouragement.

Sabina Wurmbrand could show us how to give up our pity parties and look to what God has done for us; she could show us what we can be for the glory of God.

Isobel Kuhn had this motto: GOD FIRST. Her life was devoted to her husband's missionary work in China. Surely she knew it was not the popular thing to do—devoting herself as she did to his work.

Knowing she was dying of cancer, she gave her daughter to God to be a missionary. Surely she wanted her child home with her, at least until her death. But she didn't ask for that. Rather, she sent her away, knowing Mother would never see her again in this life. Then, while on her deathbed, Isobel wrote comforting letters to sustain families of missionary martyrs.

Hers must have been a changed life forever.

Catherine Luther had a changed life. She stood by her husband in times of great discouragement. She started a ladies' visitation to comfort the sick, help the needy and take Christ to the lost. Catherine quickly turned her home into a hospital to help care for the sick during the Plague. After doing that, she had to quietly suffer through snubs and slander from the very ones she had helped! Then she turned right around and forgave those same ungrateful people when the Plague returned! This type of unselfish action is something about which we know so very little.

Let us take our example from her and forgive and love and give ourselves completely to Him and to our fellowman.

Catherine Luther's was truly a changed life forever.

They now name some girls' dormitories at Christian schools after martyred **Betty Stam.** Hers must have been a changed life. She maintained an ardent prayer life and relied completely upon Christ for strength and direction.

Betty devoted her life to serving Christ with her missionary husband, John Stam. Surely she grieved to leave behind her three-month-old baby girl to march up a hill beside her husband at the point of communist swords, to willingly kneel beside him and to become a martyr with him.

Perhaps we too will someday have to turn our backs on a beloved child and trust him/her completely to God in order to do His will.

Oh, that we would take Betty Stam as our example in order to have a changed life forever!

Georgia Creel Jones must have had a changed life. She died when her boy Bobby was very young; but she never really died. She lives on in my heart and in the hearts of thousands of students who knew her at Bob Jones University. Though she never even visited that great school, yet she was there every minute of every day for so many years.

You see, in the short time she had with her boy, she gave him some principles that somehow came through to thousands of us as her "Bobby" became Dr. Bob Jones, Sr.

Dr. Bob said many a time to the students that he would rather have had a little cabin mother without a grade school education than a so-called "great" one who had a Ph.D. but didn't know Jesus.

Mrs. Jones is living in Heaven now, but she is also living on earth because of her life, a changed life forever.

Helen Zugmier—my mom. I sometimes wonder why she told me some of the things she used to tell me. I remember her saying, "Grandma Wilkins used to say that the world dances into the church and the church dances into the world until you can't tell the difference."

I thought that was strange; I didn't understand it. I think I may have laughed when Mom told me about Grandma Wilkins.

But I wonder just how much got through to me as Mom told me about our neighbor whom everyone called "Grandma Wilkins," one of the women in my own mom's life.

I remember Mom's talking about the news coming to her that her own mother had been killed in a tragic train wreck. I never knew my grandmother, but people who did said she was a different woman and that the whole countryside mourned her death because she had been a friend to so many.

Do you suppose my life and the lives of girls in my classes are somehow being shaped by a grandmother I never knew and an elderly neighbor called Grandma Wilkins?

I remember when I was a sixth grader and some of us wanted to go to the sixth-grade dance. Mom and Dad objected. The local minister's wife called and tried to convince them they were being a little fanatical. But Mom always wanted me to be different; so somewhere along the line her life must have been changed forever.

I was just a little kid during the Depression of the 1930's, but I can remember how hard it hit the families in Nebraska. Because of the dryness, crops couldn't grow, and people had a hard time breathing because of the dust and heat.

But my Aunt Velva was the kind of person who could have a baby one day and do a big wash the next. Aunt Velva worked hard. She spent her whole lifetime caring for others. Now that she is without someone to care for, she feels a little guilty about having spare time for herself. She nursed a husband, a sister and a dad. The last two were Aunt Edna and Grandpa. She took care of all three until their deaths.

What causes a woman to do this but a life changed forever?

My Aunt Lela and Uncle Carl must have had changed lives to have taken me to Siloam Springs, Arkansas, for a Sword Conference when they didn't know a thing about the Sword of the Lord. They had only seen one copy of it, and that copy advertised a conference a long way away. They weren't the kind to just pick up and go someplace. I have no idea what could have prompted them except changed lives. They didn't know Dr. Bob Jones, Sr., or any of the others who were to be speaking there.

Perhaps they were afraid for me; perhaps they noticed a little bit of a rebellious spirit coming through. I just know that God changed their lives to make them want to do this for me.

When they took me to that Sword Conference, they changed my life forever.

I have been married to the only son of Mom Evans for over a quarter of a century now, and I think we have yet to have our first fuss. That has to be to her credit and not to mine. I'm sure there were plenty of times when she would have liked to have told me a whole lot of things to do differently, but she held her peace and waited. It seems that she always looked for the good in me and blacked out the bad.

She is an example of a changed life for many mothers-in-law of today.

I don't talk a lot anymore about having a best friend, but Annie Ruth McGuire was that to me at one time. When I first came to Hammond, she came with me since I was just four weeks out of back surgery. She always saw to it that I was taken care of and that nice things were done for me. She decorated my hospital room for my wedding anniversary when my surgery was scheduled for that date. She was always there just going along with my silly ways and being my best friend.

Her life was a changed one.

Nancy Perry kept on going when she lost her husband, home, business and health, all within a few years. I don't know how she did it. The answer must be that she had made Jesus Lord and Master of her life. She has shown a strength through all the losses that few people know anything about—much less possess.

It must all be the result of a changed life. . . a changed life forever.

And say, what about you out there? Is your life changed? Forever? It can be!

Thanks. . .

My love and gratitude to Leslie Simpson Beaman who had a dream for this book much sooner and with more intensity than I ever did.

She not only dreamed. She worked long hours over many months editing and laboriously putting the pieces together to produce a manuscript ready to send off for a reading.

SLP